HOW TO MAKE CLEAN COPIES FROM THIS BOOK

YOU MAY MAKE COPIES OF PORTIONS OF THIS BOOK WITH A CLEAN CONSCIENCE IF:

- you (or someone in your organization) are the original purchaser;
- you are using the copies you make for a noncommercial purpose (such as teaching or promoting your ministry) within your church or organization;
- you follow the instructions provided in this book.

HOWEVER, IT IS ILLEGAL FOR YOU TO MAKE COPIES IF:

- you are using the material to promote, advertise or sell a product or service other than for ministry fund-raising;
- you are using the material in or on a product for sale;
- you or your organization are **not** the original purchaser of this book.

By following these guidelines you help us keep our products affordable.
Thank you,
Gospel Light

PRAISE FOR YOUTHBUILDERS

Jim Burns knows young people. He also knows how to communicate to them. This study should be in the hands of every youth leader interested in discipling young people.

David Adams, Vice President, Lexington Baptist College

I deeply respect and appreciate the groundwork Jim Burns has prepared for true teenage discernment. YouthBuilders is timeless in the sense that the framework has made it possible to plug into any society, at any point in time, and to proceed to discuss, experience and arrive at sincere moral and Christian conclusions that will lead to growth and life changes. Reaching young people may be more difficult today than ever before, but God's grace is alive and well in Jim Burns and this wonderful curriculum.

Fr. Angelo J. Artemas, Youth Ministry Director, Greek Orthodox Archdiocese of North and South America

I heartily recommend Jim Burns's *YouthBuilders Group Bible Studies* because they are leader-friendly tools that are ready to use in youth groups and Sunday School classes. Jim addresses the tough questions that students are genuinely facing every day and, through his engaging style, challenges young people to make their own decisions to move from their current opinions to God's convictions taught in the Bible. Every youth group will benefit from this excellent curriculum.

Paul Borthwick, Minister of Missions, Grace Chapel

Jim Burns recognizes the fact that small groups are where life change happens. In this study he has captured the essence of that value. Further, Jim has given much thought to shaping this very effective material into a usable tool that serves the parent, leader and student.

Bo Boshers, Executive Director, Student Impact, Willow Creek Community Church

THE WORD ON

THE SERMON ON THE MOUNT

JIM BURNS

THE NATIONAL INSTITUTE OF YOUTH MINISTRY

Gospel Light

Gospel Light is an evangelical Christian publisher dedicated to serving the local church. We believe God's vision for Gospel Light is to provide church leaders with biblical, user-friendly materials that will help them evangelize, disciple and minister to children, youth and families.

We hope this Gospel Light resource will help you discover biblical truth for your own life and help you minister to youth. God bless you in your work.

For a free catalog of resources from Gospel Light please contact your Christian supplier or call 1-800-4-GOSPEL.

PUBLISHING STAFF
William T. Greig, Publisher
Dr. Elmer L. Towns, Senior Consulting Publisher
Dr. Gary S. Greig, Senior Consulting Editor
Jean Daly, Managing Editor
Pam Weston, Editorial Assistant
Kyle Duncan, Editorial Director
Bayard Taylor, M.Div., Editor, Theological and Biblical Issues
Joey O'Connor, Contributing Writer
Mario Ricketts, Designer

ISBN 0-8307-1723-4
© 1996 Jim Burns
All rights reserved.
Printed in U.S.A.

It is about time that someone who knows kids, understands kids and works with kids writes youth curriculum that youth workers, both volunteer and professional, can use. Jim Burns's *YouthBuilders Group Bible Studies* is the curriculum that youth ministry has been waiting a long time for.

Ridge Burns, President,
The Center for Student Missions

There are very few people in the world who know how to communicate life-changing truth effectively to teens. Jim Burns is one of the best. *YouthBuilders Group Bible Studies* puts handles on those skills and makes them available to everyone. These studies are biblically sound, hands-on practical and just plain fun. This one gets a five-star endorsement—which isn't bad since there are only four stars to start with.

Ken Davis, President,
Dynamic Communications

I don't know anyone who knows and understands the needs of the youth worker like Jim Burns. His new curriculum not only reveals his knowledge of youth ministry but also his depth and sensitivity to the Scriptures. *YouthBuilders Group Bible Studies* is solid, easy to use and gets students out of their seats and into the Word. I've been waiting for something like this for a long time!

Doug Fields, Pastor of High School,
Saddleback Valley Community Church

Jim Burns has a way of being creative without being "hokey." *YouthBuilders Group Bible Studies* takes the age-old model of curriculum and gives it a new look with tools such as the Bible *Tuck-In*™ and Parent Page. Give this new resource a try and you'll see that Jim shoots straightforward on tough issues. The *YouthBuilders* series is great for leading small-group discussions as well as teaching a large class of junior high or high school students. The Parent Page will help you get support from your parents in that they will understand the topics you

are dealing with in your group. Put Jim's years of experience to work for you by equipping yourself with this quality material.

Curt Gibson, Pastor to Junior High,
First Church of the Nazarene of Pasadena

Once again, Jim Burns has managed to handle very timely issues with just the right touch. His *YouthBuilders Group Bible Studies* succeeds in teaching solid biblical values without being stuffy or preachy. The format is user-friendly, designed to stimulate high involvement and deep discussion. Especially impressive is the Parent Page, a long overdue tool to help parents become part of the Christian education loop. I look forward to using it with my kids!

David M. Hughes, Pastor,
First Baptist Church, Winston-Salem

What do you get when you combine a deep love for teens, over 20 years' experience in youth ministry and an excellent writer? You get Jim Burns's *YouthBuilders* series! This stuff has absolutely hit the nail on the head. Quality Sunday School and small-group material is tough to come by these days, but Jim has put every ounce of creativity he has into these books.

Greg Johnson, author of *Getting Ready for the Guy/Girl Thing* and *Keeping Your Cool While Sharing Your Faith*

Jim Burns has a gift, the gift of combining the relational and theological dynamics of our faith in a graceful, relevant and easy-to-chew-and-swallow way. *YouthBuilders Group Bible Studies* is a hit, not only for teens but for teachers.

Gregg Johnson, National Youth Director,
International Church of the Foursquare Gospel

The practicing youth worker always needs more ammunition. Here is a whole book full of practical, usable resources for those facing kids face-to-face. *YouthBuilders Group Bible Studies* will get that blank stare off the faces of kids in your youth meeting!
Jay Kesler, President, Taylor University

I couldn't be more excited about the *YouthBuilders Group Bible Studies.* It couldn't have arrived at a more needed time. Spiritually we approach the future engaged in war with young people taking direct hits from the devil. This series will practically help teens who feel partially equipped to "put on the whole armor of God."
Mike MacIntosh, Pastor,
Horizon Christian Fellowship

In *YouthBuilders Group Bible Studies,* Jim Burns pulls together the key ingredients for an effective curriculum series. Jim captures the combination of teen involvement and a solid biblical perspective, with topics that are relevant and straightforward. This series will be a valuable tool in the local church.
Dennis "Tiger" McLuen, Executive Director,
Youth Leadership

My ministry takes me to the lost kids in our nation's cities where youth games and activities are often irrelevant and plain Bible knowledge for the sake of learning is unattractive. Young people need the information necessary to make wise decisions related to everyday problems. *YouthBuilders* will help many young people integrate their faith into everyday life, which after all is our goal as youth workers.
Miles McPherson, President, Project Intercept

Jim Burns's passion for teens, youth workers and parents of teens is evident in the *YouthBuilders Group Bible Studies.* He has a gift of presenting biblical truths on a

level teens will fully understand, and youth workers and parents can easily communicate.
Al Menconi, President, Al Menconi Ministries

Youth ministry curriculum is often directed to only one spoke of the wheel of youth ministry—the adolescent. Not so with this material! Jim has enlarged the education circle, including information for the adolescent, the parent and the youth worker. *YouthBuilders Group Bible Studies* is youth and family ministry-oriented material at its best.
Helen Musick, Instructor of Youth Ministry,
Asbury Seminary

Finally, a Bible study that has it all! It's action-packed, practical and biblical; but that's only the beginning. *YouthBuilders* involves students in the Scriptures. It's relational, interactive and leads kids toward lifestyle changes. The unique aspect is a page for parents, something that's usually missing from adolescent curriculum. Jim Burns has outdone himself. This isn't a home run—it's a grand slam!
Dr. David Olshine, Director of Youth Ministries,
Columbia International University

Here is a thoughtful and relevant curriculum designed to meet the needs of youth workers, parents and students. It's creative, interactive and biblical—and with Jim Burns's name on it, you know you're getting a quality resource.
Laurie Polich, Youth Director,
First Presbyterian Church of Berkeley

In 10 years of youth ministry I've never used a curriculum because I've never found anything that actively involves students in the learning process, speaks to young people where they are and challenges them with biblical truth—I'll use this! *YouthBuilders Group Bible Studies* is a complete curriculum that is helpful to parents, youth leaders and, most importantly, today's youth.

Glenn Schroeder, Youth and Young Adult Ministries, Vineyard Christian Fellowship, Anaheim

This new material by Jim Burns represents a vitality in curriculum and, I believe, a more mature and faithful direction. *YouthBuilders Group Bible Studies* challenges youth by teaching them how to make decisions rather than telling them what decisions to make. Each session offers teaching concepts, presents options and asks for a decision. I believe it's healthy, the way Christ taught and represents the abilities, personhood and faithfulness of youth. I give it an A+!

J. David Stone, President, Stone & Associates

Jim Burns has done it again! This is a practical, timely and reality-based resource for equipping teens to live life in the fast-paced, pressure-packed adolescent world of the '90s. A very refreshing creative oasis in the curriculum desert!

Rich Van Pelt, President, Alongside Ministries

YouthBuilders Group Bible Studies is a tremendous new set of resources for reaching students. Jim has his finger on the pulse of youth today. He understands their mind-sets, and has prepared these studies in a way that will capture their attention and lead to greater maturity in Christ. I heartily recommend these studies.

Rick Warren, Senior Pastor, Saddleback Valley Community Church

CONTENTS

DEDICATION

To Craig Deane,
From youth group kid to coworker in youth ministry!

    Your ministry, your lifestyle and your friendship are truly an inspiration.
Thank you for all the hours and energy you have given to NIYM and THIS SIDE UP.
Thank you for wiring the stereo!
God is using you in a hundred wonderful ways.

        You are loved and appreciated,
        Jim

"Being confident of this, that he who began a good work in you will carry it on to completion until the day of Christ Jesus" (Philippians 1:6).

THANKS AND
THANKS AGAIN!

This project is definitely a team effort. First of all, thank you to Cathy, Christy, Rebecca and Heidi Burns, the women of my life. Thank you to Jill Corey, my incredible assistant and long time friend. Thank you to Doug Webster for your outstanding job as Executive Director of NIYM. Thank you to the NIYM staff in San Clemente, Gary Lenhart, Russ Cline, Laurie Pilz, Luchi Bierbower, Dean Bruns and Larry Acosta. Thank you to our 100-plus associate trainers who have been my coworkers, friends and sacrificial guinea pigs. Thank you to Kyle Duncan, Bill Greig III and Jean Daly for convincing me that Gospel Light is a great publisher who deeply believes in the mission to reach kids. I believe! Thank you to the Youth Specialties world. Tic, Mike and Wayne, so many years ago you brought on a wet-behind-the-ears youth worker and taught me most everything I know about youth work today. Thank you to the hundreds of donors, supporters and friends of the National Institute of Youth Ministry. You are helping create an international grass-roots movement that is helping young people make positive decisions that will affect them for the rest of their lives.

"Where there is no counsel, the people fall; but in the multitude of counselors there is safety"
(Proverbs 11:14, *NKJV*).

Jim Burns
San Clemente, CA

YOUTHBUILDERS GROUP BIBLE STUDIES

It's Relational—Students learn best when they talk—not when you talk. There is always a get acquainted section in the Warm Up. All the experiences are based on building community in your group.

It's Biblical—With no apologies, this series in unashamedly Christian. Every session has a practical, relevant Bible study.

It's Experiential—Studies show that young people retain up to 85 percent of the material when they are *involved* in action-oriented, experiential learning. The sessions use role-plays, discussion starters, case studies, graphs and other experiential, educational methods. *We believe it's a sin to bore a young person with the gospel.*

It's Interactive—This study is geared to get students feeling comfortable with sharing ideas and interacting with peers and leaders.

It's Easy to Follow—The sessions have been prepared by Jim Burns to allow the leader to pick up the material and use it. There is little preparation time on your part. Jim did the work for you.

It's Adaptable—You can pick and choose from several topics or go straight through the material as a whole study.

It's Age Appropriate—In the "Team Effort" section, one group experience relates best to junior high students while the other works better with high school students. Look at both to determine which option is best for your group.

It's Parent Oriented—The Parent Page helps you to do youth ministry at its finest. Christian education should take place in the home as well as in the church. The Parent Page is your chance to come alongside the parents and help them have a good discussion with their kids.

It's Proven—This material was not written by someone in an ivory tower. It was written for young people and has already been used with them. They love it.

HOW TO USE THIS STUDY

The 12 sessions are divided into three stand-alone units. Each unit has four sessions. You may choose to teach all 12 sessions consecutively. Or you may use only one unit. Or you may present individual sessions. You know your group best so you choose.

Each of the 12 sessions is divided into five sections.

Warm Up—Young people will stay in your youth group if they feel comfortable and make friends in the group. This section is designed for you and the students to get to know each other better. These activities are filled with history-giving and affirming questions and experiences.

Team Effort—Following the model of Jesus, the Master Teacher, these activities engage young people in the session. Stories, group situations, surveys and more bring the session to the students. There is an option for junior high/middle school students and one for high school students.

In the Word—Most young people are biblically illiterate. These Bible studies present the Word of God and encourage students to see the relevance of the Scriptures to their lives.

Things to Think About—Young people need the opportunity to really think through the issues at hand. These discussion starters get students talking about the subject and interacting on important issues.

Parent Page—A youth worker can only do so much. Reproduce this page and get it into the hands of parents. This tool allows quality parent/teen communication that really brings the session home.

THE BIBLE *TUCK-IN*™

It's a tear-out sheet you fold and place in your Bible, containing the essentials you'll need for teaching your group.

HERE'S HOW TO USE IT:

To prepare for the session, first study the session. Tear out the Bible *Tuck-In*™ and personalize it by making notes. Fold the Bible *Tuck-In*™ in half on the dotted line. Slip it into your Bible for easy reference throughout the session. The Key Verse, Biblical Basis and Big Idea at the beginning of the Bible *Tuck-In*™ will help you keep the session on track. With the Bible *Tuck-In*™ your students will see that your teaching comes from the Bible and won't be distracted by a leader's guide.

Unit 1

PRIORITIES

LEADER'S PEP TALK

It's a rare occasion when I am speechless. Cathy has told me throughout our 21-plus years of marriage that I talk too much. She's right! However, there have been a few times when I was so struck with awe and amazement that I was reduced to absolute silence with a tear or two running down my cheek: the first time I held my children, standing in St. Peter's Basilica in Rome, my mother's passing from earth to eternity, when our pastor announced, "You are now man and wife" and when Babe Ruth hit the home run for the kid in the hospital. Okay. I think you have the picture. For me, that sense of amazement and awe fills my soul when I read the words of Jesus in the Sermon on the Mount.

My hope is that when you finish these sessions you and your students will have a richer faith and a deeper understanding of the core teachings of Jesus Christ. No one can study the Sermon on the Mount without having a profound respect for the Man from Galilee who gave us these words and, more importantly, lived His life according to these distinguished teachings. I believe that all who study this sermon will have the same response to it that the first listeners had almost 2000 years ago. "When Jesus had finished saying these things, the crowds were amazed at his teaching, because he taught as one who had authority, and not as their teachers of the law" (Matthew 7:28,29).

William Barclay introduced this most important message this way:

> The Sermon on the Mount is greater than we think. Matthew in his introduction wishes us to see that it is the official teaching of Jesus; that it is the opening of Jesus' whole mind to His disciples; that it is the summary of the teaching which Jesus habitually gave to His inner circle. The Sermon on the Mount is nothing less than the concentrated memory of many hours of heart to heart communion between the disciples and their Master.

My prayer is that your heart and your students' hearts will burn with a desire to be silent before the Lord and hear Him speak through these powerful words of the Sermon on the Mount.

THE BEATITUDES:
KEYS TO THE KINGDOM

(K)EY VERSES

"Now when he saw the crowds, he went up on a mountainside and sat down. His disciples came to him, and he began to teach them, saying:

'Blessed are the poor in spirit, for theirs is the kingdom of heaven.

'Blessed are those who mourn, for they will be comforted.

'Blessed are the meek, for they will inherit the earth.

'Blessed are those who hunger and thirst for righteousness, for they will be filled.

'Blessed are the merciful, for they will be shown mercy.

'Blessed are the pure in heart, for they will see God.

'Blessed are the peacemakers, for they will be called sons of God.

'Blessed are those who are persecuted because of righteousness, for theirs is the kingdom of heaven.

'Blessed are you when people insult you, persecute you and falsely say all kinds of evil against you because of me. Rejoice and be glad, because great is your reward in heaven, for in the same way they persecuted the prophets who were before you." Matthew 5:1-12

(B)IBLICAL BASIS

Psalm 1:1; 119:1-3;
Proverbs 8:32-34;
Matthew 5:1-12;
1 Corinthians 11:1

(T)HE BIG IDEA

Christians will be truly happy if they follow the teaching of Jesus in the Beatitudes.

(A)IMS OF THIS SESSION

During this session you will guide students to:
• Examine the powerful words of Jesus in the Beatitudes;
• Discover how these important statements relate to their own lives;
• Implement decisions to work toward living out the Beatitudes in their daily lives.

(W)ARM UP

SHOE RELAY—
Students race to find their own shoes.

(T)EAM EFFORT— JUNIOR HIGH/ MIDDLE SCHOOL

THE FIGHT—
A story illustrating how to live according to the Beatitudes.

(T)EAM EFFORT— HIGH SCHOOL

THE BEATITUDE CHECK-UP—
Students rate their Christlikeness.

(I)N THE WORD

THE BEATITUDES—
A Bible study on the Beatitudes.

(T)HINGS TO THINK ABOUT (OPTIONAL)

Questions to get students thinking and talking about applying the Beatitudes in real life.

(P)ARENT PAGE

A tool to get the session into the home and allow parents and young people to discuss and brainstorm how to improve on practicing the "Beatitude life."

LEADER'S DEVOTIONAL

"Follow my example, as I follow the example of Christ"
(1 Corinthians 11:1).

Are you a full-time, professional youth worker? Are you a Sunday School volunteer for your church and youth ministry? Or is this your first time preparing a Bible study for teenagers and you're scared to death? Regardless of the amount of your time or experience in ministering to teenagers, chances are you're a busy person. Trying to balance your life with work, friends, family, social events, your favorite sitcom, working out, attending youth ministry meetings, church events and yes, preparing Bible study lessons like this one, it's easy to lose perspective on why you're doing what you're doing. (Something I've done many times before!)

The Sermon on the Mount and the Beatitudes, in particular, are a great place to pull off the busy highway of life for a spiritual "Rest Area." They are a wonderful reminder about why you're doing what you're doing. I sincerely believe that by the time you finish preparing for this lesson, you'll discover new and refreshing ways Jesus wants the Beatitudes lived out in your life.

You see, in youth ministry, there is always the temptation to do more and more at the cost of spending less and less time with God. Make one more phone call. Make one more appointment. Create one more event. The Beatitudes call us to look past our "doing" and challenge us to consider who we are in Christ. They inspire us to first "be" in Christ and to rest in Him, too.

To truly make a difference in young people's lives, you and I need godly characters carved in the image of Christ. We need to be pilgrims before we are event programmers. We need to be followers before we are leaders. Teenagers respond to the changed lives of adults who sincerely and authentically love them with the love of Christ. That's something no program or event can ever do.

Before you begin to prepare for this lesson, take a few minutes to ask God for a refreshing, new perspective of His word. Ask Jesus to make the Beatitudes a reality in your life. (Written by Joey O'Connor.)

"Let us often remember, my dear friend, that our sole occupation in life is to please God. What meaning can anything else have?"
—Brother Lawrence

THE BEATITUDES: KEYS TO THE KINGDOM

KEY VERSES

"Now when he saw the crowds, he went up on a mountainside and sat down. His disciples came to him, and he began to teach them, saying:

'Blessed are the poor in spirit, for theirs is the kingdom of heaven.

'Blessed are those who mourn, for they will be comforted.

'Blessed are the meek, for they will inherit the earth.

'Blessed are those who hunger and thirst for righteousness, for they will be filled.

'Blessed are the merciful, for they will be shown mercy.

'Blessed are the pure in heart, for they will see God.

'Blessed are the peacemakers, for they will be called sons of God.

'Blessed are those who are persecuted because of righteousness, for theirs is the kingdom of heaven.

'Blessed are you when people insult you, persecute you and falsely say all kinds of evil against you because of me. Rejoice and be glad, because great is your reward in heaven, for in the same way they persecuted the prophets who were before you." Matthew 5:1-12

BIBLICAL BASIS

Psalm 1:1; 119:1-3; Proverbs 8:32-34; Matthew 5:1-12; 1 Corinthians 11:1

THE BIG IDEA

Christians will be truly happy if they follow the teaching of Jesus in the Beatitudes.

WARM UP (5-10 MINUTES)

SHOE RELAY

• Divide students into teams of five or six members each.

• Have students remove their shoes and place them in one big pile. Mix up the shoes making sure that no pairs are together.

• At an adult leader's signal each team is to send one person to the pile. He or she has to find his or her pair of shoes, put them on, tie them and then run back to the team for the next person to do the same thing. The first team to finish is the winner.

---- Fold ----

5. Merciful—Matthew 5:7: To show mercy is to extend compassion to someone without desiring to punish him or her for a wrongdoing, just as God does with us.
According to this verse, why do you think our treatment of others will affect God's treatment of us?

What are examples of acts of mercy in and around your life?

6. Pure in Heart—Matthew 5:8: The people in Jesus' day considered the heart the center of a person's being, including mind, will and emotions. To be "pure in heart" means that our thoughts, motives and reactions are pure.
Why might being "pure in heart" help you "see God"?

7. Peacemakers—Matthew 5:9: It is the Father's nature to make peace.
Why is it fitting that "the peacemakers" will be called sons of God?

How can you be a peacemaker in your home, school, church and community?

8. Persecuted—Matthew 5:10-12: Persecution is being unfairly or even cruelly treated or harassed due to one's personal beliefs.
What do you think the disciples might have felt when they heard Jesus' words as recorded in Matthew 5:10-12?

"Persecution is a terrible thing, but unfaithfulness is far worse." What is your reaction to this statement?

SO WHAT?

Which statement of the Beatitudes is the most difficult for you personally to follow?

Which statement will you begin to work on this week?

THINGS TO THINK ABOUT (OPTIONAL)

• Use the questions on page 24 after or as a part of "In the Word."

1. What do you think real happiness looks like?

2. Why do these words of Jesus in the Beatitudes seem so foreign to the modern-day advice given for success?

3. Why is it difficult to apply these Beatitudes to our lives?

PARENT PAGE

• Distribute page to parents.

MIDDLE SCHOOL (15-20 MINUTES)

THE FIGHT

• Give each student a copy of "The Fight" on pages 19 and 20, or display a copy using an overhead projector.
• Have students take turns reading the story aloud, or have an adult leader read it.
• Discuss the questions at the end.

Read The Beatitudes: Matthew 5:1-12.

How does this story summarize the important message of the Beatitudes?

What action steps will you take this week to use the Beatitudes to make a difference in your life?

Which Beatitude do you need to work on the most?

TEAM EFFORT—HIGH SCHOOL (15-20 MINUTES)

A BEATITUDE CHECK-UP

• Give each student a copy of "A Beatitude Check-Up" on page 21 and a pen or pencil.
• Have students complete the page.

Read the following statements that reflect commitment to the teaching of the Beatitudes. Then in the space by each statement, evaluate your level of commitment to each Beatitude. Rate your commitment from 1 to 10 and write that number on the line beside each statement.

1 2 3 4 5 6 7 8 9 10

A long way to go   Lukewarm   Christlike

Poor in Spirit—"I am helpless without Christ, therefore my complete trust is in Him."

Mourn—"I am truly sorry for my sin and for the suffering in the world."

Hunger and Thirst—"I desire a relationship with God more than money, people, success or anything."

Mercy—"I hurt for others, feel what they feel, think their thoughts, experience their pain."

Pure in Heart—"I have pure motives and reasons for all my actions. I don't dwell on impure thoughts."

Peacemaker—"My goal is for all my relationships with others to be completely peaceful."

Persecuted—"I obey Christ regardless of criticism, loneliness, rejection or fear."

Circle the sentence completions that apply to you.
For me to become more of a disciple of Christ, I need to....

a. obey Him more.
b. meditate on His word.
c. start a new life with Him.
d. trust Him completely.
e. choose one Beatitude and make a commitment to improve my obedience to its teaching.
f. find Christlike friends.
g. weigh the costs and pay the price.

Fold

h. put my happiness in Him, not money, health, people, etc.
i. other.

IN THE WORD (25-30 MINUTES)

THE BEATITUDES

• Divide students into groups of three or four.
• Give each student a copy of "The Beatitudes" on pages 22, 23 and 24 and a pen or pencil, or display the page using an overhead projector.
• Have students complete the Bible study.

What do these verses say about the blessedness of those who follow God?

Psalm 1:1

Psalm 119:1-3

Proverbs 8:32-34

1. Poor in Spirit—Matthew 5:3: To be "poor in spirit" is to acknowledge our spiritual poverty, our bankruptcy before God.
Why is this necessary to receive the Kingdom of Heaven?

Why do you think Jesus begins His greatest collection of teachings with "Blessed are the poor in spirit?"

Why is it so difficult to admit our spiritual poverty?

2. Mourn—Matthew 5:4: Those who mourn feel sorrow not only for their own sin but also for the sin they see around them.
What have you experienced lately that caused you to mourn?

How do you think those who mourn will be comforted?

3. Meek—Matthew 5:5: The word *meek* means to have a humble and gentle attitude toward others.
From the world's point of view, why is it surprising that the meek will inherit the earth?

What can you see in the life of Christ that exemplifies or defines meekness?

4. Hunger and Thirst—Matthew 5:6: To hunger and thirst is to urgently desire nutrition.
What does it mean to hunger and thirst for righteousness?

What is the important result of hungering and thirsting for righteousness according to this verse?

TEAM EFFORT

THE FIGHT

The following is one of the stories that has most influenced my life. It took place during World War I and was told by an old colonel in the Austrian Army.

I was commanded to march against a little town on the Tyrol and lay siege to it. We had been meeting stubborn resistance in that part of the country, but we felt sure that we should win because all of the advantages were on our side. My confidence, however, was arrested by a remark from a prisoner we had taken. "You will never take that town," he said, "for they have an invincible leader."

"What does the fellow mean?" I inquired of one of my staff. "And who is this leader of whom he speaks?"

Nobody seemed able to answer my question, and so in case there should be some truth in the report, I doubled preparations.

As we descended through the pass in the Alps, I saw with surprise that the cattle were still grazing in the valley and that women and children—yes, and even men—were working in the fields.

Either they are not expecting us, or this is a trap to catch us, I thought to myself. As we drew nearer the town we passed people on the road. They smiled and greeted us with a friendly word, and then went on their way.

Finally, we reached the town and clattered up the cobble-paved streets— colors flying, horns sounding a challenge, arms in readiness. Women came to the windows or doorways with little babies in their arms. Some of them looked startled and held their babies closer, then went quietly on with their household tasks without panic or confusion. It was impossible to keep strict discipline, and I began to feel rather foolish. My soldiers answered the questions of children, and I saw one old warrior throw a kiss to the little golden-haired tot on the doorstep. "Just the size of Lisa," he muttered. Still no sign of an ambush. We rode straight to the open square which faced the town hall. Here, if anywhere, resistance surely was to be expected.

Just as I had reached the hill and my guard was drawn up at attention, an old white-haired man, who by his insignia I surmised to be the mayor, stepped forth, followed by ten men in simple peasant costume. They were all dignified and unabashed by the armed force before them—the most terrible soldiers of the great and mighty army of Austria.

© 1996 by Gospel Light. Permission to photocopy granted.

TEAM EFFORT

He walked down the steps straight to my horse's side, and with hand extended, cried, "Welcome, brother!" One of my aides made a gesture as if to strike him down with his sword, but I saw by the face of the old mayor that this was no trick on his part.

"Where are your soldiers?" I demanded.

"Soldiers? Why, don't you know we have none?" he replied in wonderment, as though I had asked, "Where are your giants?" or "Where are your dwarfs?"

"But we have come to take this town."

"Well, no one will stop you."

"Are there none here to fight?"

At this question, the old man's face lit up with a rare smile that I will always remember. Often afterward, when engaged in bloody warfare, I would suddenly see that man's smile—and somehow, I came to hate my business. His words were simply:

"No, there is no one here to fight. We have chosen Christ for our Leader, and He taught men another way."

Read The Beatitudes: Matthew 5:1-12

How does this story summarize the important message of the Beatitudes?

....

....

....

Which Beatitude do you need to work on the most?

....

....

....

What action steps will you take this week to use the Beatitudes to make a difference in your life?

....

....

....

TEAM EFFORT

A BEATITUDE CHECK-UP

Read the following statements that reflect commitment to the teaching of the Beatitudes. Then in the space by each statement evaluate your level of commitment to each Beatitude. Rate your commitment from 1 to 10 and write that number on the line beside each statement.

1	2	3	4	5	6	7	8	9	10
A long way to go				Lukewarm					Christlike

.... Poor in Spirit—"I am helpless without Christ, therefore my complete trust is in Him."

.... Mourn—"I am truly sorry for my sin and for the suffering in the world."

.... Hunger and Thirst—"I desire a relationship with God more than money, people, success or anything."

.... Mercy—"I hurt for others, feel what they feel, think their thoughts, experience their pain."

.... Pure in Heart—"I have pure motives and reasons for all my actions. I don't dwell on impure thoughts."

.... Peacemaker—"My goal is for all my relationships with others to be completely peaceful."

.... Persecuted—"I obey Christ regardless of criticism, loneliness, rejection or fear."

Circle the sentence completions that apply to you.

For me to become more of a disciple of Christ, I need to...

a. obey Him more.

b. meditate on His word.

c. start a new life with Him.

d. trust Him completely.

e. choose one Beatitude and make a commitment to improve my obedience to its teaching.

f. find Christlike friends.

g. weigh the costs and pay the price.

h. put my happiness in Him—not money, health, people, etc.

i. other ....

IN THE WORD

THE BEATITUDES

Read Matthew 5:1-12.

The Beatitudes are eight keys to the Kingdom of God. Each of these eight statements contains more insight and truth than there is in most books. Jesus had a way of putting profound truths into simple words. In the Beatitudes we find this to be especially true. *Blessed* means happy or better yet, joyous.

What do these verses say about the blessedness of those who follow God?

Psalm 1:1 ....

....

Psalm 119:1-3 ....

....

Proverbs 8:32-34 ....

....

1. Poor in Spirit—Matthew 5:3: To be "poor in spirit" is to acknowledge our spiritual poverty, our bankruptcy before God.

Why is this necessary to receive the Kingdom of Heaven?

....

....

Why do you think Jesus begins His greatest collection of teachings with "Blessed are the poor in spirit"?

....

....

Why is it so difficult to admit our spiritual poverty?

....

....

2. Mourn—Matthew 5:4: Those who mourn feel sorrow not only for their own sin but also for the sin they see around them.

What have you experienced lately that caused you to mourn?

....

....

How do you think those who mourn will be comforted?

....

....

3. Meek—Matthew 5:5: The word *meek* means to have a humble and gentle attitude toward others.

From the world's point of view, why is it surprising that the meek will inherit the earth?

....

....

What can you see in the life of Christ that exemplifies or defines meekness?

....

....

4. Hunger and Thirst—Matthew 5:6: To hunger and thirst is to urgently desire nutrition.

What does it mean to hunger and thirst for righteousness?

....

....

What is the important result of hungering and thirsting for righteousness according to this verse?

....

....

5. Merciful—Matthew 5:7: To show mercy is to extend compassion to someone without desiring to punish him or her for a wrongdoing—just as God does with us.

According to this verse, why do you think our treatment of others will affect God's treatment of us?

....

....

What are examples of acts of mercy in and around your life?

....

....

6. Pure in Heart—Matthew 5:8: The people in Jesus' day considered the heart the center of a person's being, including mind, will and emotions. To be "pure in heart" means that our thoughts, motives and reactions are pure.

Why might being "pure in heart" help you "see God"?

....

....

7. Peacemakers—Matthew 5:9: It is the Father's nature to make peace.

Why is it fitting that "the peacemakers" will be called sons of God?

....

....

How can you be a peacemaker in your home, school, church and community?

....

8. Persecuted—Matthew 5:10-12: Persecution is being unfairly or even cruelly treated or harassed due to one's personal beliefs.

What do you think the disciples might have felt when they heard Jesus' words as recorded in Matthew 5:10-12?

....

....

"Persecution is a terrible thing but unfaithfulness is far worse." What is your reaction to this statement?

....

....

So What?
Which statement of the Beatitudes is the most difficult for you personally to follow?

....

....

Which statement will you begin to work on this week?

....

....

*T*HINGS TO THINK ABOUT

1. **What do you think real happiness looks like?**

....

....

2. **Why do these words of Jesus in the Beatitudes seem so foreign to the modern-day advice given for success?**

....

....

3. **Why is it difficult to apply these Beatitudes to our lives?**

....

....

**THE BEATITUDES:
KEYS TO THE
KINGDOM**

THE BEATITUDES

Read Matthew 5:1-12.

Send your family on a "scavenger hunt" throughout your home to come up with items which represent each of the Beatitudes listed below. Then have each family member choose one of the items that represent the Beatitude that he or she wants to work on. Have each family member put that item in a prominent place to remind him or her throughout the week. Spend time in prayer for one another. In a few days, have a time to share how each member is doing on his or her Beatitude.

Examples of items could be: "poor in spirit"—a penny, "mourn"—a facial tissue, "meek"—a child's toy, "hunger and thirst"—plate or cup, "merciful"—picture of people helping others, "pure in heart"—a heart, "peacemaker"—boxing gloves, "persecution"—a rubber band.

- "Blessed are the poor in spirit, for theirs is the kingdom of heaven" (Matthew 5:3).
- "Blessed are those who mourn, for they will be comforted" (Matthew 5:4).
- "Blessed are the meek, for they will inherit the earth" (Matthew 5:5).
- "Blessed are those who hunger and thirst for righteousness, for they will be filled" (Matthew 5:6).
- "Blessed are the merciful, for they will be shown mercy" (Matthew 5:7).
- "Blessed are the pure in heart, for they will see God" (Matthew 5:8).
- "Blessed are the peacemakers, for they will be called sons of God" (Matthew 5:9).
- "Blessed are those who are persecuted because of righteousness, for theirs is the kingdom of heaven" (Matthew 5:10).

Session 1: "The Beatitudes: Keys to the Kingdom"
Date...

SALT AND LIGHT:
A STRATEGIC INFLUENCE IN THE WORLD

KEY VERSES

"'You are the salt of the earth. But if the salt loses it saltiness, how can it be made salty again? It is no longer good for anything, except to be thrown out and trampled by men.

'You are the light of the world. A city on a hill cannot be hidden. Neither do people light a lamp and put it under a bowl. Instead they put it on its stand, and it gives light to everyone in the house. In the same way, let your light shine before men, that they may see your good deeds and praise your Father in heaven.'"
Matthew 5:13-16

BIBLICAL BASIS

Matthew 5:13-16;
Romans 5:3-5;
Philippians 2:14,15

THE BIG IDEA

When Christians present a godly, life-changing influence to others, there are eternally positive results.

AIMS OF THIS SESSION

During this session you will guide students to:
• Examine the Salt and Light Principle of influencing others for Jesus Christ;
• Discover how to be a strategic influence in the world for Jesus;
• Implement a specific plan for influencing others for Jesus Christ.

WARM UP

FUNNY BUNNY—
A rhyming word game.

TEAM EFFORT— JUNIOR HIGH/ MIDDLE SCHOOL

THE SALT AND LIGHT PRINCIPLE—
A discussion of how to be "salt and light" in life situations.

TEAM EFFORT— HIGH SCHOOL

SALT AND LIGHT AWARDS—
Students choose people who are examples of Christ to the world.

IN THE WORD

SALT AND LIGHT—
A Bible study on flavoring and illuminating the world as Christ would.

THINGS TO THINK ABOUT (OPTIONAL)

Questions to get students thinking and talking about being the Christlike flavor and light in their world.

PARENT PAGE

A tool to get the session into the home and allow parents and young people to discuss how to become God's salt and light in their neighborhoods.

LEADER'S DEVOTIONAL

"Not only so, but we also rejoice in our sufferings, because we know that suffering produces perseverance; perseverance, character; and character, hope. And hope does not disappoint us, because God has poured out his love into our hearts by the Holy Spirit, whom he has given us" (Romans 5:3-5).

Disappointment is a reality in youth ministry that most youth workers don't talk about too much. It's always easier to talk about the exciting things God is doing, where the next camp or retreat is going to be, or last night's hilarious crowd breaker. Disappointment is also something that volunteer youth workers don't receive much training in, yet knowing that teenagers will let you down from time to time can help you accept one of the frustrating realities of ministry.

So what does disappointment have to do with teaching young people that they are the salt and light of the world? The good news is that even though young people (and adults) will drop the ball, fall short, make mistakes and ultimately disappoint us, by God's grace, we are still the salt and light of the world. Even when we disappoint others, God's grace can fill in the cracks in our character.

There is a subtle temptation in youth ministry to focus on performance instead of process. Young people can and will make mistakes. The challenge of youth ministry is to walk alongside teenagers as they "work out" the process of their faith in Christ. The trick is to not let our disappointments get in the way of remembering that faith development is often a long, slow process. Remember: It is by God's grace that we are the salt and light of the world. Your students will shine their light brighter when they understand that they are under the grace of God and not a strict, legalistic law of performance. Even you will shine your light brighter as you receive and rest in God's grace...in spite of the disappointments you may face. (Written by Joey O'Connor.)

**We are told to let our light shine, and if it does, we won't need to tell anybody it does. Lighthouses don't fire cannons to call attention to their shining— they just shine.
—D.L. Moody**

SALT AND LIGHT: A STRATEGIC INFLUENCE IN THE WORLD

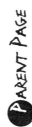

KEY VERSES

"You are the salt of the earth. But if the salt loses it saltiness, how can it be made salty again? It is no longer good for anything, except to be thrown out and trampled by men. "You are the light of the world. A city on a hill cannot be hidden. Neither do people light a lamp and put it under a bowl. Instead they put it on its stand, and it gives light to everyone in the house. In the same way, let your light shine before men, that they may see your good deeds and praise your Father in heaven." Matthew 5:13-16

BIBLICAL BASIS

Matthew 5:13-16; Romans 5:3-5; Philippians 2:14,15

THE BIG IDEA

When Christians present a godly, life-changing influence to others, there are eternally positive results.

WARM UP (5-10 MINUTES)

FUNNY BUNNY

• Give each student a copy of "Funny Bunny" on page 31 and a pen or pencil.
• Have students complete page. The first one to finish is the winner.
• Answers: 1. Far Star 2. O.K. Soufflé 3. Regal Eagle 4. Pale Nail 5. Hog Dog 6. Wood Hood 7. Fun Run 8. Bunk Junk 9. Far Car 10. Wee Flea 11. Road Toad 12. Bag Tag 13. Yellow Jello 14. Neat Seat 15. Skinny Penny 16. Main Lane 17. Chair Hair 18. Cut Nut 19. Worn Horn 20. Stick Nick 21. Broom Room 22. Snow Hoe 23. Faint Paint 24. Fat Gnat 25. Fake Lake

---- Fold ----

What would you say and do if Jesus came to you today and said, "I need you. You are my only light to your family, your friends and your school. Will you shine for me?"

So WHAT?
Who Are You Influencing?
Billy Graham, the well-known evangelist, once said, "The evangelistic harvest is always urgent. The destiny of men and nations is always being decided. Every generation is strategic. God will hold us responsible as to how well we fulfill our responsibilities to this age and take advantage of our responsibilities."
How do you feel when you hear that you are strategic for reaching your generation for God?

What can you do to fulfill your God-given responsibilities?

....

THINGS TO THINK ABOUT (OPTIONAL)
• Use the questions on page 34 after or as a part of "In the Word."
1. Why do you think light is such a common biblical image?

....

2. What makes evangelism (sharing the good news of Christ) difficult at times?

....

3. How can Christians be "light" and "salt" in your school?

....

PARENT PAGE
• Distribute page to parents.

THE SALT AND LIGHT PRINCIPLE

- Divide students into groups of three or four.
- Give each group at least one copy of "The Salt and Light Principle" on page 32, or display the page using an overhead projector.
- Have each group share its application for at least one of the situations.
- Option: Have groups role-play how they would apply "the salt and light principle" in each situation.

Read Matthew 5:13-16. In your group, discuss how you can apply "the salt and light principle" to the following situations. Be prepared to share your applications.

You are very active in your church youth group. At school you eat with the Christian Bible study students and your family is active in the church. In a Bible study on being the salt and light of the world, you have to list five non-Christian friends and you can't name one. How do you apply the salt and light principle to your life?

You are a Christian and on the junior varsity basketball team. Your teammates are friendly and fun, but they have a warped sense of humor—often using foul language and talking about sex. They constantly tell you filthy jokes and invite you to parties where there is a great deal of drinking and sexual promiscuity. What are specific ways you can apply the salt and light principle in this situation?

TEAM EFFORT—HIGH SCHOOL (15-20 Minutes)

SALT AND LIGHT AWARDS

- Give each student a copy of "Salt and Light Awards" on page 32 and a pen or pencil.
- Give students a couple of minutes to write down their own nominations for the awards.
- Divide students into groups of three or four and have them come up with a group consensus of who they would nominate for each award.
- Have each group share its list of nominees.

Just like the Emmys and Grammys, now you can create the "Salt and Light Awards." These awards go to distinguished individuals who represent a Christ-centered and Christ-glorified lifestyle. Write down who you would nominate and be prepared to share with your small group why you chose each person.

Business
Teacher
Ministry
Homemaker
Professional Athlete
Actress and/or Actor
Musician
Other:

Fold

 IN THE WORD (25-30 Minutes)

SALT AND LIGHT

- Divide students into groups of three or four.
- Give each student a copy of "Salt and Light" on pages 33 and 34 and a pen or pencil, or display the page using an overhead projector.
- Have students complete the Bible study.

Read Matthew 5:13-16.

ADDING FLAVOR AND GIVING SIGHT TO THE WORLD

In the Matthew 5:13-16 passage, what two images does Jesus use to describe His disciples?

Before refrigeration was invented, salt was used to keep meat from rotting. With this in mind, what do you think Jesus meant when He said, "You are the salt of the earth"?

What might cause Christians to lose their saltiness?

How can a Christian be a "light of the world"?

Read Philippians 2:14,15. What does Paul advise Christians to do to be lights in the world?

Why do you think "light" is such a common reference to Christ?

THE CHRISTIAN TASTE TEST

Circle the appropriate answer.
If I am salt, my relationship with Christ is...

blah   tasteless   mild   seasoned   spicy   very tasty

Complete the following sentence:
To add more "salt" to my Christian diet, I need to...

TURNED ON FOR JESUS

Circle the response that best describes you.
When it comes to shining for Christ, I...
a. shine brightly.
b. flicker now and then.
c. feel dark and cold.
d. need a new spark.
e. burn brighter every day.
f. shed light for God's glory.
g. need a few other candles for help.

**SALT AND LIGHT:
A STRATEGIC
INFLUENCE IN THE
WORLD**

FUNNY BUNNY

The left hand column has two word clues. Write the rhyming answers in the right hand column.

Clue	Answer
1. Distant Light	
2. Chef's Delight	
3. Royal Hawk	
4. White Spike	
5. Pig Chaser	
6. Log Cover	
7. Enjoyable Jog	
8. Bed Plunder	
9. Distant Auto	
10. Tiny Insect	
11. Street Frog	
12. Sack Label	
13. Lemon Dessert	
14. Tidy Chair	
15. Thin Coin	
16. Important Path	
17. Bench Fur	
18. Sliced Acorn	
19. Old Antler	
20. Branch Notch	
21. Mop Closet	
22. Ski-slope Rake	
23. Pale Watercolors	
24. Chubby Insect	
25. False Pond	

THE SALT AND LIGHT PRINCIPLE

Read Matthew 5:13-16. In your group, discuss how you can apply "the salt and light principle" to the following situations. Be prepared to share your applications.

You are a Christian and on the junior varsity basketball team. Your teammates are friendly and fun, but they have a warped sense of humor often using foul language and talking about sex. They constantly tell you filthy jokes and invite you to parties where there is a great deal of drinking and sexual promiscuity. What are specific ways you can apply the salt and light principle in this situation?

....

....

....

You are very active in your church youth group. At school you eat with the Christian Bible study students and your family is active in the church. In a Bible study on being the salt and light of the world, you have to list five *non-Christian* friends and you can't name one. How do you apply the salt and light principle to your life?

....

....

....

....

Τ EAM EFFORT

SALT AND LIGHT AWARDS

Just like the Emmys and Grammys, now you can create the "Salt and Light Awards." These awards go to distinguished individuals who represent a Christ-centered and Christ-glorified lifestyle.

Write down who you would nominate, and be prepared to share with your small group why you chose each person.

Business	....
Teacher	....
Ministry	....
Homemaker	....
Professional Athlete	....
Actress and/or Actor	....
Musician	....
Other:	....

IN THE WORD

SALT AND LIGHT

Read Matthew 5:13-16.

SALT AND LIGHT:
A STRATEGIC
INFLUENCE IN THE
WORLD

Adding Flavor and Giving Sight to the World

In the Matthew 5:13-16 passage, what two images does Jesus use to describe His disciples?

....

Before refrigeration was invented, salt was used to keep meat from rotting. With this in mind, what do you think Jesus meant when He said, "You are the salt of the earth"?

....

What might cause Christians to lose their saltiness?

....

How can a Christian be a "light of the world"?

....

Read Philippians 2:14,15. What does Paul advise Christians to do to be lights in the world?

....

Why do you think "light" is such a common reference to Christ?

....

The Christian Taste Test

Circle the appropriate answer:

If I am salt, my relationship with Christ is...

blah	tasteless	mild	seasoned	spicy	very tasty

Compete the following sentence:

To add more "salt" to my Christian diet, I need to...

....

Turned on for Jesus

Circle the response that best describes you.

When it comes to shining for Christ, I...

a. shine brightly.

b. flicker now and then.

c. feel dark and cold.

d. need a new spark.

e. burn brighter every day.

f. shed light for God's glory.

g. need a few other candles for help.

IN THE WORD

What would you say and do if Jesus came to you today and said, "I need you. You are my only light to your family, your friends and your school. Will you shine for me?"

....

....

So What?

Who Are You Influencing?

Billy Graham, the well-known evangelist, once said, "The evangelistic harvest is always urgent. The destiny of men and nations is always being decided. Every generation is strategic. God will hold us responsible as to how well we fulfill our responsibilities to this age and take advantage of our responsibilities."[1]

How do you feel when you hear that you are strategic for reaching your generation for God?

....

....

What can you do to fulfill your God-given responsibilities?

....

....

Note:

1. Billy Graham, *Quote, Unquote* (Wheaton: Victor Books, 1977) p.102.

THINGS TO THINK ABOUT

1. Why do you think light is such a common biblical image?

....

....

2. What makes evangelism (sharing the good news of Christ) difficult at times?

....

....

3. How can Christians be "light" and "salt" in your school?

....

....

SALT AND LIGHT:
A STRATEGIC
INFLUENCE IN THE
WORLD

SALT AND LIGHT
Read Matthew 5:13-16

What does salt do?

....
....
....

What does light do?

....
....

Here are three illustrations of salt and light:

1. The Jones family visits a rest home once a month. They talk with the patients, pass out Scripture and even pray with a few of the patients.

2. The Smith family brings food to the local homeless shelter and stays to help with counseling and cleaning the building.

3. The Garrity family takes care of one of their invalid neighbors. Mrs. Garrity goes shopping for her once a week. The kids take care of her lawn and Mr. Garrity makes repairs on her house.

What specifically can our family do to be salt and light to the world?

....
....
....

Session 2: "Salt and Light:
A Strategic Influence in the World"
Date...

JESUS FULFILLS THE LAW

KEY VERSES

"'Do not think that I have come to abolish the Law or the Prophets; I have not come to abolish them but to fulfill them. I tell you the truth, until heaven and earth disappear, not the smallest letter, not the least stroke of a pen, will by any means disappear from the Law until everything is accomplished. Anyone who breaks one of the least of these commandments and teaches others to do the same will be called least in the kingdom of heaven, but whoever practices and teaches these commands will be called great in the kingdom of heaven. For I tell you that unless your righteousness surpasses that of the Pharisees and the teachers of the law, you will certainly not enter the kingdom of heaven.'"
Matthew 5:17-20

BIBLICAL BASIS

Psalm 119:1-8;
Matthew 5:17-37; 12:33-37; 19:3-6;
John 14:21;
1 Corinthians 9:25-27;
James 1:19,26; 5:12

THE BIG IDEA

Righteousness is obedience to Christ in all that we think, say and do. Jesus was very clear on His interpretation of the Law.

AIMS OF THIS SESSION

During this session you will guide your students to:
• Examine the important teachings of Jesus on the law, oaths, adultery, murder and divorce;
• Discover how these teachings affect our daily lives;
• Implement a plan to live in obedience to Christ in all that we think, say and do.

WARM UP

WHY? BECAUSE...—
Students write their own questions and answers.

TEAM EFFORT— JUNIOR HIGH/ MIDDLE SCHOOL

A TRUSTWORTHY PERSON?—
A story illustrating hypocrisy.

TEAM EFFORT— HIGH SCHOOL

ANGER/LUST/DIVORCE —WHEW!—
Students examine their own thoughts on anger, lust and divorce.

IN THE WORD

THE LAW ON MURDER, ADULTERY, DIVORCE AND OATHS—
A Bible study on Jesus' directives concerning murder, adultery, divorce and oaths.

THINGS TO THINK ABOUT (OPTIONAL)

Questions to get students thinking and talking about how they can obey Jesus' words.

PARENT PAGE

A tool to get the session into the home and allow parents and young people to discuss their commitment to obeying Christ and being trustworthy.

LEADER'S DEVOTIONAL

"Everyone who competes in the games goes into strict training. They do it to get a crown that will not last; but we do it to get a crown that will last forever. Therefore I do not run like a man running aimlessly; I do not fight like a man beating the air. No, I beat my body and make it my slave so that after I have preached to others, I myself will not be disqualified for the prize"
(1 Corinthians 9:25-27).

In my first year of youth ministry, I coached a boys' junior varsity volleyball team at the same high school I attended. Since I wasn't permitted to just walk on a public campus as a youth worker, being a volleyball coach enabled me to coach a number of guys not only in the fundamentals of volleyball, but also in the fundamentals of the Christian faith. Though winning was important, my higher goal was to coach my team on how to win at life by following God's way.

Jesus' teachings on oaths, adultery, murder and divorce are clearly designed to help us win at life. These teachings are a few of the fundamentals God has outlined for our own good and protection. Just as a volleyball court has specific lines to show whether the ball is in- or out-of-bounds, God has given us His word to show us how to live within the freedom and safety of His commands.

How many students in your youth ministry have been hurt by broken marriage oaths, adultery and divorce? Countless marriages have failed because of the decisions of some parents not to follow God's fundamental commands for life. Young people need to be reassured that God's commands are given for their safety, protection and well-being. That's just one of the reasons why your ministry is so important!

This lesson is a good reminder (to us as well) about the purpose of God's commands. They are written so we can walk in peace and security with Christ. This lesson will also provide the opportunity to talk with your students about the sensitive topics of adultery, divorce and the importance of keeping our commitments. It's filled with great ideas on how to coach young people to stay inbounds for God. It will teach them that the only way to win at life is by winning God's way. (Written by Joey O'Connor.)

"Every great person has first learned how to obey, whom to obey, and when to obey."
—William Willard

JESUS FULFILLS THE LAW

KEY VERSES

"Do not think that I have come to abolish the Law or the Prophets; I have not come to abolish them but to fulfill them. I tell you the truth, until heaven and earth disappear, not the smallest letter, not the least stroke of a pen, will by any means disappear from the Law until everything is accomplished. Anyone who breaks one of the least of these commandments and teaches others to do the same will be called least in the kingdom of heaven, but whoever practices and teaches these commands will be called great in the kingdom of heaven. For I tell you that unless your righteousness surpasses that of the Pharisees and the teachers of the law, you will certainly not enter the kingdom of heaven." Matthew 5:17-20

BIBLICAL BASIS

Psalm 119:1-8; Matthew 5:17-37; 19:3-6; 5:12; John 14:21; 1 Corinthians 9:25-27; James 1:19,26

THE BIG IDEA

Righteousness is obedience to Christ in all that we think, say and do. Jesus was very clear on His interpretation of the Law.

WARM UP (5-10 MINUTES)

WHY? BECAUSE...

- Give each student a pen or pencil and two 3x5-inch cards.
- Have them write out a question beginning with the word "why" on the first card. Then on the second card have them write an answer to their question beginning with the word "because."
- Collect the question cards and then the answer cards. Keeping the questions separate from the answers, redistribute them at random so that each student has one question card and one answer card.
- Have each student read the question card and then the answer card that was given to him or her. This experience will have some funny moments.

TEAM EFFORT—JUNIOR HIGH/MIDDLE SCHOOL (15-20 MINUTES)

A TRUSTWORTHY PERSON?

- Read the following story to the whole group.

- Fold -

What does Jesus say should take place before worship?

What are the results of uncontrolled anger?

ADULTERY
Read Matthew 5:27-30.
How does Jesus define adultery?

Jesus' point in verses 29 and 30 is that we should deal drastically with sin as it is necessary. He is not teaching self-mutilation, for even a blind person can lust. How would you put verses 29 and 30 into modern language?

DIVORCE
Read Matthew 5:31-32.
What do you think Jesus is trying to say about the sanctity of marriage in verses 31 and 32?

Read Matthew 19:3-6. Jesus quotes from the book of Genesis in this passage. What point do you think He is making about God's original design for marriage?

Many wonderful people, both parents and kids, have been through hurtful divorces. What action steps can you take that might help keep divorce out of your own future marriage?

OATHS
Read Matthew 5:33-37.
What do you think Jesus meant by "swearing"?

Why do people feel the need to swear or promise?

So WHAT?
Which of these areas from these Scriptures do you need the most work on?

THINGS TO THINK ABOUT (OPTIONAL)

- Use the questions on page 46 after or as a part of "In the Word."
1. How do Jesus' words make obedience to Him more challenging than merely obeying the law?

2. How can the experiences of adultery or divorce break our relationships with God?

How can one find forgiveness in the midst of divorce and/or adultery?

3. What is the source of our righteous behavior?

PARENT PAGE
- Distribute page to parents.

• Discuss their answers to the question.
How does this man's behavior illustrate someone who seems to be living a moral life on the outside but really is not a trustworthy person?

TEAM EFFORT—HIGH SCHOOL (15-20 MINUTES)
ANGER/LUST/DIVORCE—WHEW!
• Give each student a copy of "Anger/Lust/Divorce—Whew!" on pages 42 and 43 and a pen or pencil.
• Have students complete their papers by themselves.
• Discuss appropriate portions of the questions with the whole group.

OBEDIENCE AND ANGER—MATTHEW 5:21-26
Jesus made some very strong and important statements about anger in this section of Scripture. People express anger in different ways. Which response best describes your method of venting anger? Circle the appropriate response(s).

Anger seems to surface in my life in the following way(s):
1. Yelling and screaming
2. Sarcasm and criticizing
3. Backbiting
4. Silent withdrawal or depression
5. Physical outbursts
6. Physical illness
7. Destroyed self-image
8. I have never been angry (denial).
9. Other:

What can you do to better manage your anger?

If we are to take the words of Jesus seriously, we must repair any damaged relationships with others before we attempt to worship God.
Is there someone in your life that you need to restore a broken relationship with? Who is this person? What steps do you need to take to patch up your relationship?

OBEDIENCE AND LUST—MATTHEW 5:27-30
Circle the response that best describes you.
When Jesus talks about lust, I...
1. get bored because it's not an issue for me.
2. become nervous because He's talking about me.
3. feel guilty because I've thought like that.
4. am anxious to ask forgiveness one more time.
5. am motivated to find support from other Christians.
6. want to read God's Word to clear my mind.

Fold

Why do you think this area of our lives is difficult to discuss with other Christians?

Here are a few action steps to take if lust is a problem for you:
1. Renew your mind with Scripture.
2. Change your setting or situation.
3. Seek support from a close Christian friend. Ask for prayer.
4. Take your mind off the sin by serving in the name of Christ.
5. Ask God for forgiveness.
6. Find a task that will care for someone else's needs.

OBEDIENCE AND MARRIAGE—MATTHEW 5:31,32
In what ways might divorce reveal the hardness of our hearts?

How does Jesus' teaching contrast with today's view on marriage and divorce?

How will a love relationship between two Christians who put God first in their lives be stronger than the relationships of people who do not invite God to be a part of their relationships?

What does this seem to imply for Christians who are seriously dating non-Christians?

IN THE WORD (25-30 MINUTES)
THE LAW ON MURDER, ADULTERY, DIVORCE AND OATHS
• Divide students into groups of three or four.
• Give each student a copy of "The Law on Murder, Adultery, Divorce and Oaths" on pages 44 and 45 and a pen or pencil, or display the page using an overhead projector.
• Have students complete the Bible study.

THE FULFILLMENT OF THE LAW
Read Matthew 5:17-20.
What was Jesus' view of the Old Testament laws and prophets?

What role does obedience to the law play in establishing the least and greatest in God's eyes?

Read Psalm 119:1-8. Describe the psalmist's attitude about God's laws.
How does Jesus' view of the Pharisees in Matthew 12:33-37 help you understand 5:20?

MURDER
Read Matthew 5:21-26.
What three types of "attitude murder" does Jesus mention?

**JESUS FULFILLS
THE LAW**

A TRUSTWORTHY PERSON?

A fellow went into a fried chicken place and bought a couple of chicken dinners for himself and his date late one afternoon. The young woman at the counter inadvertently gave him the proceeds for the day—a whole bag of money (much of it cash) instead of fried chicken.

After driving to their picnic site, the two of them sat down to open the meal and enjoy some chicken together. They discovered a whole lot more than chicken—over $800. But he was unusual. He quickly put the money back in the bag. They got back into the car and drove all the way back. Mr. Clean got out, walked in and became an instant hero.

By then, the manager was frantic. The guy with the bag of money looked at the manager and said, "I want you to know I came by to get a couple of chicken dinners and wound up with all this money. Here." Well, the manager was thrilled to death. He said, "Oh great, let me call the newspaper. I'm gonna have your picture put in the local paper. You're one of the most honest men I've ever heard of." To which the guy quickly responded, "Oh no, no, no, don't do that! You see, the woman I'm with is not my wife...she's uh, somebody else's wife."[1]

How does this man's behavior illustrate someone who seems to be living a moral life on the outside but really is not a trustworthy person?

....

....

....

Note:

1. Charles Swindoll, *Growing Deep in the Christian Life* (Portland: Multnomah Press, 1986), pp. 159-160.

T EAM EFFORT

ANGER/LUST/DIVORCE—WHEW!

Obedience and Anger—Matthew 5:21-26

Jesus made some very strong and important statements about anger in this section of Scripture. People express anger in different ways. Which response best describes your method of venting anger? Circle the appropriate response(s).

Anger seems to surface in my life in the following way(s):

1. Yelling and screaming
2. Sarcasm and criticizing
3. Backbiting
4. Silent withdrawal or depression
5. Physical outbursts
6. Physical illness
7. Destroyed self-image
8. I have never been angry...(denial)
9. Other:...

What can you do to better manage your anger?

....

....

If we are to take the words of Jesus seriously, we must repair any damaged relationships with others before we attempt to worship God.

Is there someone in your life that you need to restore a broken relationship with? Who is this person? What steps do you need to take to patch up your relationship?

....

....

Obedience and Lust—Matthew 5:27-30

Circle the responses that best describe you.

When Jesus talks about lust I...

1. get bored because it's not an issue for me.
2. become nervous because He's talking about me.
3. feel guilty because I've thought like that.
4. am anxious to ask forgiveness one more time.
5. am motivated to find support from other Christians.
6. want to read God's Word to clear my mind.

Why do you think this area of our lives is difficult to discuss with other Christians?

....

....

Here are a few action steps to take if lust is a problem for you:

1. Renew your mind with Scripture.
2. Change your setting or situation.
3. Seek support from a close Christian friend. Ask for prayer.
4. Take your mind off the sin by serving in the name of Christ.
5. Ask God for forgiveness.
6. Find a task that will care for someone else's needs.

Obedience and Marriage

In what ways might divorce reveal the hardness of our hearts?

....

....

How does Jesus' teaching contrast with today's view on marriage and divorce?

....

....

How will a love relationship between two Christians who put God first in their lives be stronger than the relationships of people who do not invite God to be a part of their relationships?

....

....

....

What does this seem to imply for Christians who are seriously dating non-Christians?

....

....

....

⬤N THE WORD

THE LAW ON MURDER, ADULTERY, DIVORCE AND OATHS

The Fulfillment of the Law

Read Matthew 5:17-20.

What was Jesus' view of the Old Testament laws and prophets?

....

....

What role does obedience to the Law play in establishing the least and greatest in God's eyes?

....

....

Read Psalm 119:1-8. Describe the psalmist's attitude about God's laws.

....

....

How does Jesus' view of the Pharisees in Matthew 12:33-37 help you understand 5:20?

....

....

Murder

Read Matthew 5:21-26.

What three types of "attitude murder" does Jesus mention?

....

....

What does Jesus say should take place before worship?

....

....

What are the results of uncontrolled anger?

....

....

Adultery

Read Matthew 5:27-30.

How does Jesus define adultery?

....

....

Jesus' point in verses 29 and 30 is that we should deal drastically with sin as it is necessary. He is not teaching self-mutilation, for even a blind person can lust. How would you put verses 29 and 30 into modern language?

....

....

Divorce

Read Matthew 5:31-32.
What do you think Jesus is trying to say about the sanctity of marriage in verses 31 and 32?

....

....

Read Matthew 19:3-6. Jesus quotes from the book of Genesis in this passage. What point do you think He is making about God's original design for marriage?

....

....

Many wonderful people, both parents and kids, have been through hurtful divorces. What action steps can you take that might help keep divorce out of your own future marriage?

....

....

Oaths

Read Matthew 5:33-37.

What do you think Jesus meant by "swearing"?

....

....

Why do people feel the need to swear or promise?

....

....

So What?

Which of these areas from these Scriptures do you need the most work on?

....

....

....

*T*HINGS TO *T*HINK *A*BOUT

1. How do Jesus' words make obedience to Him more challenging than merely obeying the law?

   ....

   ....

2. How can the experiences of adultery or divorce break our relationships with God?

   ....

   ....

   ....

   How can one find forgiveness in the midst of divorce and/or adultery?

   ....

   ....

   ....

3. What is the source of our righteous behavior?

   ....

   ....

   ....

JESUS FULFILLS THE LAW

OBEDIENCE ACCORDING TO JESUS

Read Matthew 5:17-37.

Although our salvation and grace are free gifts from God, commitment to Christ can be very costly. In this section of Scripture, Jesus calls His followers to a deeper commitment to obedience. Where are you on the obedience scale?

On a scale of one to ten, ten being the highest, I rate my obedience to God as a _____.

Carefully read John 14:21.

According to this verse, how should we show God we love Him?

....

What will He do in response to our obedience?

....

Obedience and Your Word

You've probably heard people described as men or women of their word. This means that their word can be trusted.

Are you a person who is trustworthy? Put a mark on the line above the word that best describes your degree of trustworthiness.

....

Seldom   **Sometimes**   **Most of the time**   **Always**

Read James 5:12.
What keeps people from simply saying "yes" or "no"?

....

....

According to James 5:12 and Matthew 5:37, what is the result of disobedience in this area?

....

....

How can the advice given in James 1:19 and 1:26 help you to be trustworthy?

....

....

What are your thoughts about this principle?

....

....

....

....

....

There are times when many Christians say, "If only God would reveal more of Himself, I would obey Him." According to John 14:21 the opposite is true. He reveals more of Himself to those who love and obey Him.

Here is a great spiritual principle to remember:

If you love God, you will obey Him, and He promises to reveal Himself to you!

Session 3: "Jesus Fulfills the Law"
Date ....

LOVING THE UNLOVABLE

KEY VERSES

"'You have heard that it was said, "Love your neighbor and hate your enemy." But I tell you: Love your enemies and pray for those who persecute you.'" Matthew 5:43,44

BIBLICAL BASIS

Leviticus 24:17-20;
Proverbs 20:22;
Jeremiah 11:18-20;
Matthew 5:38-48;
Luke 9:51-56;
John 8:1-11; 15:13;
Acts 7:59—8:1;
Romans 5:10; 12:20;
1 Corinthians 4:12,13

THE BIG IDEA

Jesus Christ compels us to love other people, even those we simply do not like and those who are our enemies.

AIMS OF THIS SESSION

During this session you will guide students to:
• Examine their attitudes toward their enemies and those they would call unlovable;
• Discover the biblical challenge to love the unlovable;
• Implement a lifestyle of loving those we call our enemies and those who have offended us.

WARM UP

THE SALESPERSON—
Students try to sell an unknown product.

TEAM EFFORT— JUNIOR HIGH/ MIDDLE SCHOOL
ANGUS MCGILLIVRAY—
A story of how one man's sacrifice transformed prisoners in a prisoners-of-war camp.

TEAM EFFORT— HIGH SCHOOL
GETTING EVEN—
A story and discussion of the desire for revenge and Jesus' teaching on taking revenge.

IN THE WORD

AN EYE FOR AN EYE AND LOVE YOUR ENEMIES—
A Bible study on how to deal with unlovable people in a Christlike way.

THINGS TO THINK ABOUT (OPTIONAL)
Questions to get students thinking and talking about the difficulties of loving their enemies.

PARENT PAGE
A tool to get the session into the home and allow parents and young people to discuss revenge and how to apply Jesus' teaching to real-life situations.

LEADER'S DEVOTIONAL

"On the contrary: 'If your enemy is hungry, feed him; if he is thirsty, give him something to drink. In doing this, you will heap burning coals on his head'" (Romans 12:20).

Teaching teenagers a Bible study on loving enemies is relatively easy in comparison to doing it. Perhaps, that's why James said that few of us should aspire to be teachers?

Who are the unlovables in your life right now? Who are the kids or adults that drive you crazy? Who are the people you feel like grabbing by the collar and screaming, "If you do that one more time, I'm gonna knock you into next week?" What types of personalities or attitudes annoy you like a mosquito in your face on a sleepless night at 3:00 A.M.? Or worse, who are your enemies, the bile-producing adversaries you lock horns with in mortal combat?

One of the biggest challenges any student in your youth ministry, you or I will ever face is learning how to love our enemies. An enemy is the last thing most of us would want to have. And loving an enemy is the last thing most of us would want to do. Loving the unlovable people in our lives requires a motivation and strength that comes from God. How else could we possibly do it?

I don't know about you, but there are people in my life that just bug me. When I'm really honest with myself and truthful with God, I have no real desire to love or be with people who irritate me. That's why I need God's grace to do what I can't do in my own human strength. I know He can give me the humility and grace to love others in spite of myself.

I'd venture to say that loving your enemies is the true evidence of a transformed life—a real conversion of human nature. That's the direction this lesson is pointing us—in the direction of loving others as Jesus does. (Written by Joey O'Connor.)

**"The best way to destroy your enemy is to make him your friend."
—Abraham Lincoln**

Tear along perforation. Fold and place this Bible *Tuck-In*™ in your Bible for session use.

LOVING THE UNLOVABLE

KEY VERSES

"You have heard that it was said, "Love your neighbor and hate your enemy." But I tell you: Love your enemies and pray for those who persecute you.'" Matthew 5:43,44

BIBLICAL BASIS

Leviticus 24:17-20; Proverbs 20:22; Jeremiah 11:18-20; Matthew 5:38-48; Luke 9:51-56; John 8:1-11; 15:12; Acts 7:59—8:1; Romans 5:10; 12:20; 1 Corinthians 4:12,13

THE BIG IDEA

Jesus Christ compels us to love other people, even those we simply do not like and those who are our enemies.

WARM UP (5-10 MINUTES)

THE SALESPERSON

• Choose three students who are potential salespeople. Take them out of the room and explain to them that they will be selling a product to the group and that they should try their best to answer all the questions from the group. The "salespeople" will not know what product they will be selling! At the same time, tell the rest of the group that each salesperson will be selling toilet paper and that they can ask any question they want to about this product. Also tell them that the salespeople have no idea that the product they are selling is toilet paper—so warn them not to use the specific word "toilet paper" as they ask questions. (It's a set up for fun and you are sure to get some laughs).

TEAM EFFORT—JUNIOR HIGH/

MIDDLE SCHOOL (15-20 MINUTES)

ANGUS McGILLIVRAY

• Divide students into groups of three or four.
• Give each student a copy of "Angus McGillivray" on page 53, or display the page using an overhead projector.
• Have students read the story and discuss their answers to the question.

----- Fold -----

51

Circle the response that best applies to you.

Enemies—What enemies?
a. Overwhelmed
b.
c. Excited
d. Challenged
e. Guilty
f. Impossible!
g. Encouraged

SO WHAT?

Who do you think of when you hear the words of Jesus, "love your enemies"? Take a step of courage and list the name(s) below. (Use initials if this information is too personal.)

What specific steps can you take to love your enemies?

Now take a moment to look back over your list of enemies and pray for each person. Ask God to soften your heart toward them and their hearts toward you and God. Don't be surprised to see major changes in your relationship with your enemy!

THINGS TO THINK ABOUT (OPTIONAL)

• Use the questions on page 57 after or as a part of "In the Word."

1. On a scale of 1-10 (10 being the highest) how radical are these words of Jesus?
___ a. "Love your enemies"   ___ b. "Turn the other cheek"

2. What makes someone an enemy?

3. What is the difficult part of turning the other cheek?

PARENT PAGE

• Distribute page to parents.

How could your commitment to living out God's love transform your world?

Team Effort—High School (15-20 Minutes)

Getting Even

- Divide students into groups of three or four.
- Give each student a copy of "Getting Even" on pages 54 and 55 and a pen or pencil, or display the page using an overhead projector.
- Have students complete their pages and discuss their answers in their groups.

How would you feel about using Berman's service?

Has someone taken revenge on you? Explain.

Read Matthew 5:38-48. When someone wrongs you, is your first reaction to demand an "eye for an eye" or do you "turn the other cheek"? Explain.

Berman says her business gives people a "way to vent things out." Is this a healthy or unhealthy vent for anger? Explain.

Is it realistic for human beings to love their enemies? Why or why not?

Jesus said we're supposed to "be perfect, therefore, as your heavenly Father is perfect" (Matthew 5:48). What kind of perfection is Jesus talking about?

Read Romans 5:10. Are you an enemy or a friend of God right now? If God operated according to the goals of "Enough is Enough," what would be different about your life?

When you hurt God by your actions, does he ever take revenge on you? Why or why not?

What's the difference between revenge and discipline? Explain.

In The Word (25-30 Minutes)

AN EYE FOR AN EYE AND LOVE YOUR ENEMIES

- Divide students into groups of three or four.
- Give each student a copy of "An Eye for an Eye and Love Your Enemies" on pages 56 and 57 and a pen or pencil, or display the page using an overhead projector.
- Have students complete the Bible study.

A New Understanding of Revenge—Matthew 5:38-42
Read Matthew 5:38-42. Read Leviticus 24:17-20. How might a primarily Jewish crowd with an understanding of Leviticus and the Law react to hearing Jesus preach this part of the Sermon on the Mount? What do you think Jesus is saying in verses 38-42?

Why is it difficult to do as Proverbs 20:22 says when you feel as if you have been wronged?

What positive steps can you take to become a person who follows the teaching recorded in Matthew 5:38-42?

Love Your Enemies—Matthew 5:43-48
Read Matthew 5:43-48.
What do you think Jesus meant when He said, "Love your enemies?"

Read Acts 7:59,60. What did Stephen do when he was being stoned by the religious leaders?

According to Acts 8:1, who was present at Stephen's death?

Read Matthew 5:44. How do you see Stephen living out this Scripture?

Do you think Stephen's prayer affected Saul (Paul)?

Read 1 Corinthians 4:12,13. How did Paul apply the words of Jesus from Matthew 5:44?

Why is it logical for "Love your enemies" (v. 44) and "Be perfect...as your heavenly Father is perfect" (v. 48) to be together in the same paragraph?

TURNING THE OTHER CHEEK
Complete the following sentences.
To me, "Turn the other cheek" means...

The most difficult part of turning the other cheek is...

LOVING THE UNLOVABLE
The words of Jesus in Matthew 5:44-48 are some of the Bible's most profound and radical. They are also among the most difficult words to live out.
How do you feel when you hear the words of Jesus, "Love your enemies"?

LOVING THE UNLOVABLE

ANGUS McGILLIVRAY

Read and discuss the following story.

Angus was a Scottish prisoner in one of the camps filled with Americans, Australians and Britons who had helped build the Bridge over the River Kwai. The camp had become an ugly situation. A dog-eat-dog mentality had set in. Allies would literally steal from each other and cheat each other; men would sleep on their packs and yet have them stolen from under their heads. Survival was everything. The law of the jungle prevailed...until the news of Angus McGillivray's death spread throughout the camp. Rumors spread in the wake of his death. No one could believe big Angus had succumbed. He was strong, one of those whom they had expected to be the last to die. Actually it wasn't the fact of his death that shocked the men, but the reason he died. Finally they pieced together the true story.

The...Scottish soldiers took the buddy system very seriously. Their buddy was called their "mucker," and these soldiers believed that it was literally up to each of them to make sure their "mucker" survived. Angus's mucker, though, was dying, and everyone had given up on him, everyone of course, but Angus. He had made up his mind that his friend would not die. Someone had stolen his mucker's blanket. So Angus gave him his own, telling his mucker that he had "just come across an extra one." Likewise every mealtime, Angus would get his rations and take them to his friend, stand over him and force him to eat them, and again stating that he was able to get "extra food." Angus was going to do anything and everything to see that his buddy got what he needed to recover.

But as Angus's mucker began to recover, Angus collapsed, slumped over and died. The doctors discovered that he had died of starvation complicated by exhaustion. He had been giving of his own food and shelter. He had given everything he had—even his own life. The ramifications of his acts of love and unselfishness had a startling impact on the compound. "Greater love has no one than this, that he lay down his life for his friends" (John 15:13).

As word circulated of the reason for Angus McGillivray's death, the feel of the camp began to change. Suddenly, men began to focus on their mates, their friends, the humanity of living beyond survival, of giving oneself away. They began to pool their talents—one was a violin maker, another an orchestra leader, another a cabinet maker, another a professor. Soon the camp had an orchestra full of homemade instruments and a church called "Church Without Walls" that was so powerful, so compelling, that even the Japanese guards attended. The men began a university, a hospital, and a library system. The place was transformed; an all but smothered love revived, all because one man named Angus gave all he had for his friend. For many of those men this turnaround meant survival. What happened is an awesome illustration of the potential unleashed when one person actually gives it all away.[1]

How could your commitment to living out God's love transform your world?

....

....

....

....

....

....

....

....

Note:

1. Tim Hansel, *Holy Sweat* (Waco: Word Books, 1987), pp. 146,147.

GETTING EVEN
Company Helps People Get Even With Enemies

Newton, Mass.—If you're a spurned lover or a frustrated employee, Nan Berman has some advice for you: Don't get mad, get even. Berman has a business called Enough is Enough, billed as "Creative Revenge for Today's World." Berman has mailed a 3-foot dead bluefish to an unfaithful husband in California and delivered a burned and messy suit to a lawyer who implied his girlfriend was "unsuitable."

The most common requests, however, are for 13 dead roses sent in a black box ($25) and 13 black balloons tied together by a single black rose ($30). Other "insults to suit the occasion" include a real stuffed shirt ($25) for pompous employers and drinking glasses with cigarette butts on the bottom for smokers.

Berman says: "Twenty years ago, people didn't speak up the way they do now. But since the '60's, people have expressed themselves. With me, you really have a way to vent things out."

The 43-year-old Berman started Enough Is Enough after she spent a year driving a florist delivery truck for a boss who was "the grumpiest most unpleasant person ever born."

Berman promises her customers anonymity. "I want to stress that we'll do anything, as long as it's legal," she says.[1]

Has someone taken revenge on you? Explain.

....

....

....

How would you feel about using Berman's service?

....

....

....

LOVING THE UNLOVABLE

Read Matthew 5:38-48. When someone wrongs you, is your first reaction to demand "an eye for an eye" or do you "turn the other cheek"? Explain.

....
....
....

Berman says her business gives people a "way to vent things out." Is this a healthy or unhealthy vent for anger? Explain.

....
....

Is it realistic for human beings to love their enemies? Why or why not?

....
....

Jesus said we're supposed to "be perfect, therefore, as your heavenly Father is perfect" (Matthew 5:48). What kind of perfection is Jesus talking about?

....
....

Read Romans 5:10. Are you an enemy or a friend of God right now? If God operated according to the goals of "Enough is Enough," what would be different about your life?

....
....

When you hurt God by your actions, does He ever take revenge on you? Why or why not?

....
....

What's the difference between revenge and discipline? Explain.

....
....
....

Note:

1. *Headline News Discussion Starters* (Loveland, CO: Group Books) p. 92.

IN THE WORD

AN EYE FOR AN EYE AND LOVE YOUR ENEMIES

A New Understanding of Revenge—Matthew 5:38-42

Read Matthew 5:38-42.

Read Leviticus 24:17-20. How might a primarily Jewish crowd with an understanding of Leviticus and the Law react to hearing Jesus preach this part of the Sermon on the Mount?

....

What do you think Jesus is saying in verses 38-42?

....

Why is it difficult to do as Proverbs 20:22 says when you feel as if you have been wronged?

....

What positive steps can you take to become a person who follows the teaching recorded in Matthew 5:38-42?

....

Love Your Enemies—Matthew 5:43-48

Read Matthew 5:43-48.

What do you think Jesus meant when He said, "Love your enemies"?

....

Read Acts 7:59,60. What did Stephen do when he was being stoned by the religious leaders?

....

According to Acts 8:1, who was present at Stephen's death?

....

Read Matthew 5:44. How do you see Stephen living out this Scripture?

....

Do you think Stephen's prayer affected Saul (Paul)?

....

Read 1 Corinthians 4:12,13. How did Paul apply the words of Jesus from Matthew 5:44?

....

Why is it logical for "Love your enemies" (v. 44) and "Be perfect...as your heavenly Father is perfect" (v. 48) to be together in the same paragraph?

....

Turning the Other Cheek

Complete the following sentences.

To me, "Turn the other cheek" means...

....

The most difficult part of turning the other cheek is...

....

Loving the Unlovable

The words of Jesus in Matthew 5:44-48 are some of the Bible's most profound and radical. They are also among the most difficult words to live out.

How do you feel when you hear the words of Jesus, "Love your enemies?"

....

....

Circle the response that best applies to you.

a. Enemies—What enemies?
b. Overwhelmed
c. Excited
d. Challenged
e. Guilty
f. Impossible!
g. Encouraged

So What?

Who do you think of when you hear the words of Jesus, "Love your enemies"? Take a step of courage and list the name(s) below. (Use initials if this information is too personal.)

....

....

....

What specific steps can you take to love your enemies?

....

....

....

....

Now take a moment to look back over your list of enemies and pray for each person. Ask God to soften your heart toward them and their hearts toward you and God. Don't be surprised to see major changes in your relationship with your enemy!

THINGS TO THINK ABOUT

1. On a scale of 1-10 (10 being the highest) how radical are these words of Jesus?

.... a. "Love your enemies"

.... b. "Turn the other cheek"

2. What makes someone an enemy?

....

....

....

3. What is the difficult part of turning the other cheek?

....

....

....

....

....

 PARENT PAGE

REVENGE—ENEMIES AND OUR RESPONSE

Read John 8:1-11. Who did the adulterous woman hurt by her actions?

....

Who was the only one in the crowd with a true "right of revenge"?

....

How do you feel about Jesus' response to the situation?

....

....

Since the woman wasn't punished, do you think she will commit adultery again? Why or why not?

....

....

Read Luke 9:51-56. What was the disciples' attitude toward their enemies?

....

....

Why did Jesus rebuke them?

....

....

Read Jeremiah 11:18-20. Was Jeremiah right for asking God to take vengeance on his enemies? Why or why not?

....

....

Are you taking revenge when you ask God to deal with your enemies? Why or why not?

....

....

Who are your family's enemies right now?

....

....

What can you, as a family, do to change that situation?

....

....

Session 4: "Loving the Unlovable"
Date ....

MOTIVES

LEADER'S PEP TALK

My Mom died this year. It was cancer, and it was not a pleasant experience. Mom was truly a hero in my life and yet her influence had little to do with her beauty, intelligence or sense of humor. Mom had pure motives. I don't meet many people with pure motives these days. One of my constant prayers for myself is "God, help me to not have mixed motives." This section of the Sermon on the Mount deals with motives—pure motives.

Mom was sick in bed for several months before she died. I would go over to the house almost every day. Usually, I would just sit in her room or get her something to eat. Dad would wait on her, wait on me and watch ball games on TV.

One day I was sitting in a chair in the bedroom with Mom when she looked up at me and said "Jimmy, where's your Dad?"

"He's in the living room watching a ball game, Mom," I answered. That's where he spent most of his time.

Mom then looked up at me and said, "I never really liked baseball much."

"Mom, you never liked baseball? Did you ever miss even one of my Little League, Pony League, junior high or high school baseball games?" I was absolutely shocked that she would say that after all those years of watching my games and my brothers' games. She would sit with Dad for hours and watch ball games.

"No, Jimmy. I never much cared for that sport. I didn't go to the games to watch baseball. I went to support you."

Wow, after all those years she told me she didn't even like the game. Her motive for watching ball games was far beyond enjoying the sport.

It was the power of being there. She was present at those games for me.

This section of the Sermon on the Mount challenges us to live with a higher call and purer motives than the world does. It talks about some "where-the-rubber-meets-the-road" issues like handling money, judging others and worrying about material possessions. Jesus' teachings go against the grain of the culture while presenting an eternal perspective.

What a privilege we have to place in the lives of these kids eternal truth from the mouth of Jesus. Thanks for doing what you do. And thanks for the power of being there for the kids. Your very presence makes a difference, and your motives teach your students more than you will ever imagine.

TESTING OUR MOTIVES

K EY VERSE

"'Be careful not to do your "acts of righteousness" before men, to be seen by them. If you do, you will have no reward from your Father in heaven.'" Matthew 6:1

B IBLICAL BASIS

1 Kings 18:26,29;
Psalm 120:2; 139:23,24;
Matthew 4:2; 6:1-18; 17:21; 23:1-7;
Mark 2:18-20; 11:25,26;
Luke 18:9-14;
2 Corinthians 8:8,9; 9:6-8;
Colossians 3:23;
1 Timothy 4:7

T HE BIG IDEA

Jesus teaches the importance of a right motive to support right spiritual action.

A IMS OF THIS SESSION

During this session you will guide students to:
• Examine their motives;
• Discover the biblical teachings on motives;
• Implement a decision to integrate right motives with right spiritual action.

W ARM UP

THE GREAT PYRAMID RACE—

A race that takes teamwork to win.

T EAM EFFORT— JUNIOR HIGH/ MIDDLE SCHOOL

THE LORD'S PRAYER—

Students put the Lord's Prayer into their own words.

T EAM EFFORT— HIGH SCHOOL

THE SPIRITUAL DISCIPLINES QUIZ—

Students test their knowledge of the disciplines of giving, praying and fasting.

I N THE WORD

GIVING, PRAYING AND FASTING—

A Bible study on the right and wrong motives for giving, praying and fasting.

T HINGS TO THINK ABOUT (OPTIONAL)

Questions to get students thinking and talking about their own motives for various spiritual activities.

P ARENT PAGE

A tool to get the session into the home and allow parents and young people to discuss and apply the disciplines of giving, praying and fasting.

LEADER'S DEVOTIONAL

"Search me, O God, and know my heart; test me and know my anxious thoughts. See if there is any offensive way in me, and lead me in the way everlasting" (Psalm 139:23,24).

"Why are you involved in youth ministry?" Ask any youth worker this question and you're bound to get a number of socially acceptable, spiritually-correct answers based on apparently good and pure motives.

• I want to see kids come to Christ.

• I have a drug background and I don't want teenagers to make the same mistakes I did.

• My youth minister had a big impact on my life. I want to do the same for others.

• No one else volunteered to work with the teenagers in our church.

What some of us youth workers, though, won't readily admit to is that some of our motives may not be so pure. My motives are not always pure. My motives do not always honor God. Is this shocking? I don't think so. If we're really honest with one another, we'd admit to one another that there is a dark side of ministry shadowed by impure motives, self-seeking ambition, misguided emotional needs and, at times, simplistic answers to very complicated problems.

The truthful reality of living in a broken world is that everyone, whether Christian or not, must balance between the delicate scales of pure and impure motives. That's why this lesson on motives is so important to Jesus. As new creations in Christ, God is calling you and I to walk in truth with pure motives. To do so, we need the help of the Holy Spirit to sift through the inner lives of our hearts. We need God's grace to ferret out anything in our characters that misrepresents the person God wants us to be. It's a process that begins with such simple, beautiful prayers like The Lord's Prayer.

Through Jesus Christ, we don't live under guilt or condemnation because of what our motives are or aren't. We have access to our Heavenly Father who will gently purify, clarify and direct our hearts to ministering out of honest and authentic motives. That's what we really need. Honest! (Written by Joey O'Connor.)

"People are always motivated by at least two reasons: the one they tell you about and a secret one."
—O.A. Batista

TESTING OUR MOTIVES

KEY VERSES

"Be careful not to do your "acts of righteousness" before men, to be seen by them. If you do, you will have no reward from your Father in heaven." Matthew 6:1

BIBLICAL BASIS

1 Kings 18:26,29; Psalm 120:2; 139:23,24; Matthew 4:2; 6:1-18; 17:21; Mark 2:18-20; 11:25,26; Luke 18:9-14; 2 Corinthians 8:8,9; 9:6-8; Colossians 3:23; 1 Timothy 4:7

THE BIG IDEA

Jesus teaches the importance of a right motive to support right spiritual action.

WARM UP (5-10 MINUTES)

THE GREAT PYRAMID RACE

- Divide students into groups of six each. They must then build a pyramid of three people on the bottom, two on the middle level and one on top. Then they must race to a designated spot. If the pyramid collapses before reaching the goal, they must stop and rebuild before continuing. Take the necessary precautions to insure this is a safe activity.
- If you have a small youth group with only enough for one pyramid, have them race against time.

TEAM EFFORT—JUNIOR HIGH/ MIDDLE SCHOOL (15-20 MINUTES)

THE LORD'S PRAYER

- Divide students into groups of three or four.
- Give each student a copy of "The Lord's Prayer" on page 65 and a pen or pencil.
- Have students complete the activity.
  Write in your own words each line of the Lord's Prayer (Matthew 6:9-13) and then share your words with your group.
  "Our Father in heaven,—
  hallowed be your name,—

What does this prayer tell us about God?

What does this prayer tell us about what we should say to God?

Write down the five most important people, things and/or activities in your life. Then number them in order of importance to you with 1 being the most important.

Now evaluate your list in light of what you believe would most glorify God. Do you think your priorities are pleasing to Him? Why or why not?

What do you need to change in order to bring more glory to God?

What decisions and action steps will you need to take to begin the process of putting these priorities in proper order in your life?

SO WHAT?

List below the areas of your life in which fasting would be beneficial in order to get your priorities straight. Remember: These areas are not necessarily evil, they just keep us from being all that God wants us to be.

THINGS TO THINK ABOUT (OPTIONAL)

- Use the questions on page 70 after or as a part of "In the Word."
1. How important in your spiritual life are the disciplines of giving, praying and fasting?

2. Why does forgiveness from the Father seem to have as a condition our forgiveness of other people?

3. What is your motive for the following activities:
Going to church—
Praying—
Giving—
Helping other people—

PARENT PAGE

- Distribute page to parents.

your kingdom come,—
your will be done—
on earth as it is in heaven.—

Give us today our daily bread.—

Forgive us our debts,—

as we also have forgiven our debtors.—

And lead us not into temptation,—

but deliver us from the evil one.' "—

 ## TEAM EFFORT—HIGH SCHOOL (15-20 MINUTES)

THE SPIRITUAL DISCIPLINES QUIZ

• Give each student a copy of "The Spiritual Disciplines Quiz" on page 66 and a pen or pencil.
• Give students a few minutes to complete the quiz by themselves, then take a few minutes to discuss their answers.

Answer the following questions by writing "Agree" or "Disagree" beside each statement.

_____ A person is very spiritual if he or she gives at least 10 percent of his or her income to God.

_____ A person is not very spiritual if he or she does not spend a regular daily time with God in prayer.

_____ When Paul said to Timothy "Discipline yourself for the purpose of godliness" (1 Timothy 4:7, *NASB*), he was making a very important statement about our spiritual growth.

_____ It's wrong to get recognition for giving money to the church for charity.

_____ Prayer in private is often more powerful than prayer in public.

_____ Fasting is a lost spiritual discipline that can have a great deal of value for today's Christian.

 ## IN THE WORD (25-30 MINUTES)

GIVING, PRAYING AND FASTING

• Divide students into groups of three or four.
• Give each student a copy of "Giving, Praying and Fasting," on pages 67, 68, 69 and 70 and a pen or pencil, or display the page using an overhead projector.
• Have students complete the Bible study.

Read Matthew 6:1-4.
What label does Jesus give to those who draw attention to their giving?

According to Colossians 3:23, what is to be the motivation for all our work?

Read Matthew 6:5-15.
In verses 5 through 8 Jesus taught His disciples how not to pray. List the "how-not-tos" given in these verses.

What did Jesus do after He taught the disciples how not to pray?

Take some time to look at the Lord's Prayer (vv. 9-13). Use the following spaces to list the important attitudes, priorities and requests you discover in the prayer.

Attitudes:

Priorities:

Requests:

Why do you think Jesus followed the prayer with the statement found in verses 14 and 15?

Read Matthew 6:16-18.
Notice that Jesus did not say *if* you fast; He said *when* you fast. He assumed that His followers would fast. What advice about fasting does Jesus give in verses 16 through 18?

What is fasting?

"Fasting is the act of temporarily giving up something that is very important to us in order that we may use the time normally given to that thing for prayer and reflection upon the pain of the temporary 'sacrifice' to better understand the mystery and meaning of Christ's passion and sacrifice for us."

Circle the response that describes your feeling at this time.
When it comes to giving up food as a Christian discipline, I...
a. would be interested in trying it.
b. would be sacrificing a lot.
c. have never tried it.
d. consider it a regular part of my spiritual growth.
e. don't know.

What three things did Jesus say to do in secret?

Why do you think He said this?

In what areas of your life are you tempted to seek the approval of people rather than of God?

What did Jesus mean when He said, "But when you give to the needy, do not let your left hand know what your right hand is doing" (Matthew 6:3)?

How can this passage help purify our motives?

TESTING OUR MOTIVES

THE LORD'S PRAYER

Write each line of the Lord's Prayer (Matthew 6:9-13) in your own words and then share your words with your group.

"'Our Father in heaven,– ....

....

hallowed be your name,– ....

....

your kingdom come,– ....

....

your will be done– ....

....

on earth as it is in heaven.– ....

....

Give us today our daily bread.– ....

....

Forgive us our debts,– ....

....

as we also have forgiven our debtors.– ....

....

And lead us not into temptation,– ....

....

but deliver us from the evil one.'"– ....

....

TEAM EFFORT

THE SPIRITUAL DISCIPLINES QUIZ

Answer the following questions by writing "Agree" or "Disagree" beside each statement.

.... A person is very spiritual if he or she gives at least 10 percent of his or her income to God.

.... A person is not very spiritual if he or she does not spend a regular daily time with God in prayer.

.... When Paul said to Timothy "Discipline yourself for the purpose of godliness" 1 Timothy 4:7, *NASB*), he was making a very important statement about our spiritual growth.

.... It's wrong to get recognition for giving money to the church for charity.

.... Prayer in private is often more powerful than prayer in public.

.... Fasting is a lost spiritual discipline that can have a great deal of value for today's Christian.

 N THE WORD

GIVING, PRAYING AND FASTING

To the Jews in the days of Jesus, there were three great pillars of spiritual life—giving to the needy, prayer and fasting. Jesus did not dispute the importance of these disciplines. What troubled Him was that so often the right things were done for the wrong reasons. In this section of Scripture, Jesus gave very radical teachings about these three important disciplines. He emphasized the importance of right motives.

Put Your Money Where Your Mouth Is—Matthew 6:1-4

Read Matthew 6:1-4.
What label does Jesus give to those who draw attention to their giving?

....

....

According to Colossians 3:23, what is to be the motivation for all our work?

....

....

Praying Jesus' Way—Matthew 6:5-15

Read Matthew 6:5-15.
In verses 5 through 8 Jesus taught His disciples how not to pray. List the "how-not-tos" given in these verses.

....

....

What did Jesus do after He taught the disciples how not to pray?

....

....

Take some time to look at the Lord's Prayer (vv. 9-13). Use the following spaces to list the important attitudes, priorities and requests you discover in the prayer.

Attitudes: ....

....

Priorities: ....

....

Requests: ....

....

# IN THE WORD

Why do you think Jesus followed the prayer with the statement found in verses 14 and 15?

....

....

The Fast Break—Matthew 6:16-18

Read Matthew 6:16-18.

Notice that Jesus did not say *if* you fast; He said *when* you fast. He assumed that His followers would fast. What advice about fasting does Jesus give in verses 16 through 18?

....

....

What is fasting?

> "Fasting is the act of temporarily giving up something that is very important to us in order that we may use the time normally given to that thing for prayer and reflection upon the pain of the temporary 'sacrifice' to better understand the mystery and meaning of Christ's passion and sacrifice for us."[1]

Circle the response that describes your feeling at this time:
When it comes to giving up food as a Christian discipline, I...

      a. would be interested in trying it.
      b. would be sacrificing a lot.
      c. have never tried it.
      d. consider it a regular part of my spiritual growth.
      e. don't know.

THE SCRIPTURE AND YOU

Testing Your Motives

So much of our lives is guided by secret motives. Many a person has made what appeared to be a good decision for the wrong reason and eventually became extremely unhappy. This section of Scripture in Matthew 6:1-18 reminds us to test our motives.

What three things did Jesus say to do in secret?

....

....

Why do you think He said this?

....

....

In what areas of your life are you tempted to seek the approval of people rather than of God?

....

....

IN THE WORD

What did Jesus mean when He said, "But when you give to the needy, do not let your left hand know what your right hand is doing" (Matthew 6:3)?

....

....

How can this passage help purify our motives?

....

....

Proper Motives in Prayer

The Lord's Prayer (Matthew 6:9-13) is the model Jesus gave us for prayer. We can better understand the heart and soul of Jesus through His example of how to pray with proper motives. For anyone desiring an intimate relationship with God, a closer look at this prayer will be of great benefit.

What does this prayer tell us about God?

....

....

What does this prayer tell us about what we should say to God?

....

....

How does this prayer compare to your prayers?

....

....

Getting Your Priorities Straight

It's so easy to let the truly important issues of life get out of focus. If you are like most of us, you tend to put off dealing with the most significant priorities and spend most of your time on the less important, minor issues of life.

Write down the five most important people, things and/or activities in your life. Then number them in order of importance to you with 1 being the most important.

....

....

....

Now evaluate your list in light of what you believe would most glorify God. Do you think your priorities are pleasing to Him? Why or why not?

....

....

What do you need to change in order to bring more glory to God?

....

....

IN THE WORD

What decisions and action steps will you need to take to begin the process of putting these priorities in proper order in your life?

....

....

Fasting may help you achieve your desire to get your priorities straight. Remember, fasting can be more than not eating food. Fasting is an exercise to deprive one's self of the normal and pleasant performances of life for the sake of personal enrichment and dedication to God.

You may need to fast from things that take your focus away from putting God first in your life. This could be a boyfriend, girlfriend, a car, a sport, partying or any other thing that has displaced God's rightful position.

You can fast for as short as one hour or for as long as forever.

So What?

List below the areas of your life in which fasting would be beneficial in order to get your priorities straight. Remember: These areas are not necessarily evil, they just keep us from being all that God wants us to be.

....

....

Note:

1. Reuben P. Job and Norman Shawchuck, *A Guide to Prayer* (Nashville: The Upper Room, 1983), p. 9.

THINGS TO THINK ABOUT

1. How important in your spiritual life are the disciplines of giving, praying and fasting?

....

....

2. Why does forgiveness from the Father seem to have as a condition our forgiveness of other people?

....

....

3. What is your motive for the following activities?

Going to church– ....

Praying– ....

Giving– ....

Helping other people– ....

TESTING OUR
MOTIVES

Parent Page

A Bible Study on Giving, Praying and Fasting

Giving
Read the following passages together:
> Luke 18:9-14
> 2 Corinthians 9:6-8

After reading these Scriptures, what are your conclusions about giving ?

....

....

Are there any steps our family can take to follow these Scriptures more effectively?

....

....

Praying
Read the following passages together:
> Mark 11:25,26
> Psalm 120:2
> 1 Kings 18:26,29

After reading these Scriptures, what are your conclusions about praying?

....

....

Are there any steps our family can take to follow these Scriptures more effectively?

....

....

Fasting
Read the following passages together:
> Isaiah 58:5-7
> Mark 2:18-20

After reading these Scriptures, what are your conclusions about fasting?

....

....

Are there any steps our family can take to follow these Scriptures more effectively?

....

....

Session 5: "Testing Our Motives"
Date ....

MONEY:
LIVING IN A MATERIAL WORLD

KEY VERSES

"'Do not store up for yourselves treasures on earth, where moth and rust destroy, and where thieves break in and steal. But store up for yourselves treasures in heaven, where moth and rust do not destroy, and where thieves do not break in and steal. For where your treasure is, there your heart will be also.

"'No one can serve two masters. Either he will hate the one and love the other, or he will be devoted to the one and despise the other. You cannot serve both God and Money.'"
Matthew 6:19-21,24

BIBLICAL BASIS

2 Samuel 11;
Proverbs 11:4;
Matthew 6:19-24;
1 Timothy 6:9,10;
1 Peter 5:2;
1 John 2:15-17

THE BIG IDEA

People spend money on the items that mean the most to them. Jesus commands believers to serve God and place trust in Him and not to serve or trust money.

AIMS OF THIS SESSION

During this session you will guide students to:
• Examine what Jesus taught about money and God;
• Discover how to make God, not money, their focus in life;
• Implement a decision to make their spiritual treasure a first priority.

WARM UP

FUNNY BUNNY II—
A rhyming word game.

TEAM EFFORT— JUNIOR HIGH/ MIDDLE SCHOOL

WHAT WOULD YOU DO FOR MONEY?—
Students consider what they would do for money.

TEAM EFFORT— HIGH SCHOOL

MONEY AND YOU—
A discussion on the importance of money.

IN THE WORD

TREASURES IN HEAVEN
A Bible study on making God the focus of life for believers.

THINGS TO THINK ABOUT (OPTIONAL)

Questions to get students thinking and talking about what their hearts treasure.

PARENT PAGE

A tool to get the session into the home and allow parents and young people to discuss the influence of television on their lives.

LEADER'S DEVOTIONAL

"Be shepherds of God's flock that is under your care, serving as overseers—not because you must, but because you are willing, as God wants you to be; not greedy for money, but eager to serve"
(1 Peter 5:2).

A few years ago, there was a student named Scott in our ministry whose father had died in a car crash when Scott was a little boy. The party responsible for the crash established a trust fund for the boy and his family. And then that money, a very large amount of money, accrued interest for the next fourteen years—compounded interest.

When Scott turned eighteen, he became legally responsible for all the money in his trust fund—several hundred thousand dollars' worth! He immediately went out and bought a fast new car. He bought his friends all sorts of expensive items—free meals, free movie tickets, free trips. Scott's friends enjoyed hanging out with him. Scott had so much money he didn't know what to do with it all, so he blew it.

Last I heard, Scott had spent most of his money, not bothering to invest it or even save it for a rainy day. No matter how he spent it, chances are it didn't buy him much happiness. It couldn't buy him the father he wished he could have had.

Maybe that's a story you'll want to tell the students in your youth ministry as you work through this lesson on money. This lesson will help your students evaluate what's really important in life. It begs the question for all of us, "What is really most important to me?" As a youth worker, you're definitely not in youth ministry for the money (unless you've discovered a get-rich-quick-in-youth-ministry scheme that the rest of us haven't!). Why do you spend hour after hour with teenagers?

You and your students might be surprised how important the subject of money is to Jesus. There are more verses in the Bible that talk about money, finances, investing and using our resources for God than other well-known subjects like love, grace or forgiveness. God has a lot to say about money because He knows how quickly it can steal our hearts. You'll find plenty of money matters and questions about the true treasures of our hearts in this lesson. Your time and energy preparing this lesson is a great investment with eternal returns. (Written by Joey O'Connor.)

"When I have any money I get rid of it as quickly as possible, lest it find a way into my heart."
—John Wesley

MONEY:
LIVING IN A MATERIAL WORLD

KEY VERSES

"Do not store up for yourselves treasures on earth, where moth and rust destroy, and where thieves break in and steal. But store up for yourselves treasures in heaven, where moth and rust do not destroy, and where thieves do not break in and steal. For where your treasure is, there your heart will be also.

"No one can serve two masters. Either he will hate the one and love the other, or he will be devoted to the one and despise the other. You cannot serve both God and Money.'"
Matthew 6:19-21,24

BIBLICAL BASIS

2 Samuel 11; Proverbs 11:4; Matthew 6:19-24; 1 Timothy 6:9,10; 1 Peter 5:2; 1 John 2:15-17

THE BIG IDEA

People spend money on the items that mean the most to them. Jesus commands believers to serve God and place trust in Him and not to serve or trust money.

WARM UP (5-10 Minutes)
FUNNY BUNNY II

• Give each student a copy of "Funny Bunny II" on page 77 and a pen or pencil.
• Have students complete page. The first one finished is the winner.
• Answers: 1. Dim Swim 2. Flake Rake 3. Narrow Arrow 4. Tire Fire 5. Damp Stamp 6. Middle Fiddle 7. Hat Pat 8. Moon Swoon 9. Plain Train 10. Certain Curtain 11. Right Night 12. Mixer Fixer 13. Mail Pail 14. Salad Ballad 15. Slow Tow 16. Towel Trowel 17. Long Song 18. Cute Suit 19. Farm Alarm 20. Snack Sack 21. Wheel Squeal 22. Hill Spill 23. Sign Line 24. Trail Gale 25. Blank Plank

---- Fold ----

SO WHAT?
What Will It Take?
Read the entire passage of Matthew 6:19-24 again. In your own words, write out what it will take to...
Make your spiritual treasure first priority.

Keep your eyes on the light.

Serve God and not money.

THINGS TO THINK ABOUT (OPTIONAL)

• Use the questions on page 81 after or as a part of "In the Word."
1. What makes money such a treasure?

2. Why does Jesus connect the heart with the treasure?

3. Why do so few people treasure that which moths or thieves cannot destroy or steal?

What does that phrase mean and how can you apply it to your spiritual life?

PARENT PAGE

• Distribute page to parents.

MIDDLE SCHOOL (15-20 Minutes)

WHAT WOULD YOU DO FOR MONEY?

- Begin by asking the students in your group to volunteer to tell their most embarrassing moment. Let them know that the group will decide which story is the best one and the winner will receive $5.00.
- While students are thinking of their most embarrassing moment, give each of them a copy of "What Would You Do for Money?" on page 78 and a pen or pencil. Have them complete the page in preparation for discussion following the questions.

Circle your answer(s) to each of the following questions.
Would you break the law for...
Would you cheat on a test for...

$.25?
$10?
$100?
$1000?
$10,000?

Would you give $10 to...

The best grade in the class?
A new car?
Tickets to a sold-out concert by your favorite performer(s)?
A friend?
A homeless person?
Hungry children in Africa?
A person who wants the money to buy alcohol?

TEAM EFFORT—HIGH SCHOOL (15-20 Minutes)

MONEY AND YOU

- Give each student a copy of "Money and You" on page 79, or display the page using an overhead projector.
- Divide students into groups of three or four.
- Have students discuss the page in their small groups.

Money can buy medicine, but not health.
Money can buy a house, but not a home.
Money can buy companionship, but not friends.
Money can buy entertainment, but not happiness.
Money can buy food, but not an appetite.
Money can buy a bed, but not sleep.

Money can buy a crucifix, but not a Savior.
Money can buy the good life, but not eternal life.

How do these words and the words of Jesus in Matthew 6:19-21,24 influence your view on money and things of this world?

Read Matthew 6:21,24. How are these words the opposite of what our society preaches?

IN THE WORD (25-30 Minutes)

TREASURES IN HEAVEN

- Divide students into groups of three or four.
- Give each student a copy of "Treasures in Heaven" on pages 80 and 81 and a pen or pencil, or display the page using an overhead projector.
- Have students complete the Bible study.

Read Matthew 6:19-24.

MAKE GOD YOUR TREASURE

What do you think Jesus meant when He said, "where your treasure is, there your heart will be also"?

What do the following Scriptures say about wealth and money?
Proverbs 11:4

1 Timothy 6:9,10

MAKING GOD THE FOCUS OF YOUR LIFE

According to Matthew 6:22,23, what could be the result of keeping your eyes focused on sinful things?

How does the story of David and Bathsheba (see 2 Samuel 11) prove these words of Jesus to be true?

MAKE GOD YOUR MASTER

Why do you think Jesus refers to money or riches as a "master"?

Read 1 John 2:15-17. What three worldly sins does John mention?

How do these sins relate to the words of Jesus in Matthew 6:19-24?

MONEY: LIVING IN A
MATERIAL WORLD

WARM UP

FUNNY BUNNY II
The left hand column is made up of two word clues. Write the rhyming answers in the right hand column.

Clue	Answer
1. Dark Plunge	
2. Snow Hoe	
3. Thin Spear	
4. Burning Wheel	
5. Wet Postage	
6. Center Violin	
7. Cap Tap	
8. Satellite Faint	
9. Ordinary Locomotive	
10. Specific Drapes	
11. Correct Evening	
12. Blender Repairer	
13. Letter Bucket	
14. Lettuce Song	
15. Pokey Pull	
16. Dishcloth Shovel	
17. Lengthy Melody	
18. Attractive Outfit	
19. Ranch Siren	
20. Cookie Bag	
21. Tire Noise	
22. Mountain Fall	
23. Poster Sentence	
24. Path Wind	
25. Plain Board	

TEAM EFFORT

WHAT WOULD YOU DO FOR MONEY?

Circle your answer(s) to each of the following questions.

Would you break the law for...

$.25?

$10?

$100?

$1000?

$10,000?

Would you cheat on a test for...

$1?

The best grade in the class?

A new car?

Tickets to a concert by your favorite performer(s)?

Would you give $10 to...

A friend?

A homeless person?

Hungry children in Africa?

A person who wants the money to buy alcohol?

MONEY: LIVING IN A MATERIAL WORLD

TEAM EFFORT

MONEY AND YOU

Think about money in this way:

      Money can buy medicine, but not health.
      Money can buy a house, but not a home.
      Money can buy companionship, but not friends.
      Money can buy entertainment, but not happiness.
      Money can buy food, but not an appetite.
      Money can buy a bed, but not sleep.
      Money can buy a crucifix, but not a Savior.
      Money can buy the good life, but not eternal life.[1]

How do these words and the words of Jesus in Matthew 6:19-21,24 influence your view on money and things of this world?

....

....

....

Read Matthew 6:21,24. How are these words the opposite of what our society preaches?

....

....

....

Note:

1. Charles Swindoll, *Strengthening Your Grip* (Waco: Word Books, 1982), pp. 84,85.

 N THE WORD

TREASURES IN HEAVEN
Read Matthew 6:19-24.

Make God Your Treasure

What do you think Jesus meant when He said, "where your treasure is, there your heart will be also?"

....

....

What do the following Scriptures say about wealth and money?

Proverbs 11:4

....

....

1 Timothy 6:9,10

....

....

Making God the Focus of Your Life

According to Matthew 6:22,23, what could be the result of keeping your eyes focused on sinful things?

....

....

How does the story of David and Bathsheba (2 Samuel 11) prove these words of Jesus to be true?

....

....

Make God Your Master

Why do you think Jesus refers to money or riches as a "master"?

....

....

Read 1 John 2:15-17. What three worldly sins does John mention?

....

....

How do these sins relate to the words of Jesus in Matthew 6:19-24?

....

....

**MONEY: LIVING IN A
MATERIAL WORLD**

So What?
What Will It Take?

Read this entire section of Scripture (Matthew 6:19-24) again. In your own words, write out what it will take to...

Make your spiritual treasure first priority. ....
....

Keep your eyes on the light. ....
....

Serve God and not money. ....
....

THINGS TO THINK ABOUT

1. What makes money such a treasure?
....
....

2. Why does Jesus connect the heart with the treasure?
....
....

3. Why do so few people treasure that which moths or thieves cannot destroy or steal?
....
....

   What does that phrase mean and how can you apply it to your spiritual life?
....
....

MONEY: LIVING IN A MATERIAL WORLD

Session 6: "Money: Living in a Material World"

Date ....

PARENT PAGE

TV AND THE FAMILY

One of the most powerful influences in the modern world is television. The average American home has the TV on over eight hours a day with little thought to what is being watched.

Read Matthew 6:22,23 and comment on how TV can be a negative influence in your life.

....

....

George Gerbner, the Dean of Annenberg School of Communications at the University of Pennsylvania, outlines five functions that religion formerly provided for society and that the secular electronic media now provides:

1. Television is ritual—most people watch TV not by the program but by the clock.

2. Television is institutionalized—a group of about 100 people in Hollywood produce more than 95 percent of the programs.

3. Television is uniting—most children watch what adults watch.

4. TV is compelling—most people watch religiously because it provides them a reward. It makes people feel good.

5. Television is primarily a socializing factor—it teaches children and adults certain assumptions about life.

Discuss how these five functions are affecting life today.

How do these five functions help you understand the importance of what Jesus was teaching in Matthew 6:22,23?

....

....

Complete this sentence:
For me to have better control of my spiritual walk in regard to TV's influence on my life, I need to...

....

....

What decisions could our family make about the use and abuse of TV in our family life?

....

....

TRUST VERSUS ANXIETY

KEY VERSES

"'Therefore do not worry about tomorrow, for tomorrow will worry about itself. Each day has enough trouble of its own.'" Matthew 6:34

BIBLICAL BASIS

Proverbs 12:25;
Matthew 6:25-34; 7:7-11;
Hebrews 11:1,6

THE BIG IDEA

Put Jesus Christ as the center of your trust and He will take care of your needs.

AIMS OF THIS SESSION

During this session you will guide students to:
• Examine the concept of "putting God first" in their lives;
• Discover what putting their trust in Christ means and how to do it;
• Implement a plan to lay aside their anxieties by putting their faith in Christ and asking Him to care for their needs.

WARM UP

I'M TAKING A TRIP—
A game to break the ice.

TEAM EFFORT— JUNIOR HIGH/ MIDDLE SCHOOL

A SCAVENGER HUNT FOR TRUST—
Students take a walk to look for evidence of God's care.

TEAM EFFORT— HIGH SCHOOL

DON'T WORRY!—
A skit and discussion about anxiety.

IN THE WORD

DO NOT WORRY—
A Bible study on trusting God for everything.

THINGS TO THINK ABOUT (OPTIONAL)

Questions to get students thinking and talking about worry in their own lives.

PARENT PAGE

A tool to get the session into the home and allow parents and young people to discuss faith.

LEADER'S DEVOTIONAL

"An anxious heart weighs a man down, but a kind word cheers him up" (Proverbs 12:25).

Have you noticed lately how worried and anxious teenagers are about their lives? A twelve-year-old boy worries about wearing the wrong colors of clothes to school for fear of being shot. A freshman girl in high school begins taking PSAT courses for fear of not getting into the right college. A scared senior thinks about cheating on a test for fear of not graduating. A fourteen-year-old girl constantly worries how her mom is after her parents' recent divorce. Doesn't this sound familiar? I'm sure you could fill in the blanks with plenty of other stories of the teenagers you know who carry similar burdens.

But let's talk about you for a minute. What anxieties are you facing right now in your life? What struggles and burdens are you carrying all by yourself? A very difficult aspect of youth ministry is having to prepare and speak about topics you are currently wrestling with like worry, trust and faith. For instance, you may be between jobs right now and you are anxious about how long you can make it before your funds dry up. Or you may be in conflict with another church staff member and you're constantly worrying about what you say and do in front of him or her. Or you may have just balanced your checkbook and you're wondering why you're spending so much "free" time with teenagers when what you really need is a second job.

My prayer for you as you prepare this lesson is that you come to a deeper knowledge of God and His faithfulness as a provider. The Lord knows your every need. He sees inside your heart. He knows the troubled thoughts in your mind. He knows your checkbook balance. He never intended to tell us not to be worried or anxious without intending to give us His peace. His peace is something your students need, you need, I need, we all need. (Written by Joey O'Connor.)

"Anxiety is the result of doing our own thing, on our own timing and with our resources."
—Lloyd John Ogilvie

TRUST VERSUS ANXIETY

K EY VERSES

"'Therefore do not worry about tomorrow, for tomorrow will worry about itself. Each day has enough trouble of its own.'" Matthew 6:34

B IBLICAL BASIS

Proverbs 12:25; Matthew 6:25-34; 7:7-11; Hebrews 11:1,6

T HE BIG IDEA

Put Jesus Christ as the center of your trust and He will take care of your needs.

W ARM UP (5-10 MINUTES)

I'M TAKING A TRIP

This is an easy warm up that is a sure winner to get the students to have some fun.

• A leader starts by saying "I'm taking a trip and I'm bringing _____." He or she can bring anything as long as it is only one word. The second person repeats the sentence including the first person's item and adds one more item to the list. The third person repeats the first two items and adds another item and the game continues.

• Option: As a get-acquainted game start the game by saying "Hi! My name is _____ and I'm going on a trip and I'm bringing _____."

T EAM EFFORT—JUNIOR HIGH/
MIDDLE SCHOOL (15-20 MINUTES)

A SCAVENGER HUNT FOR TRUST

Most of Jesus' teaching took place outdoors. It is difficult to envision some of the examples Jesus used in Matthew 6:25-34 if you are sitting in your house or in a church building. This is an activity to overcome this obstacle.

• Divide students into small groups of five or six and go for a walk. Look for birds flying in the air or resting on the limbs of a tree. Look for flower gardens. Stop and smell the roses. Use the sights as living messages of God's care for you. Give students a time limit of about 10 minutes.

SO WHAT?

Finish the following sentence:
Since God is able to care for the needs of the flowers and birds, then He is definitely able to care for my needs in the areas of...

....

T HINGS TO THINK ABOUT (OPTIONAL)

• Use the questions on page 90 after or as a part of "In the Word."

1. Why is it difficult to trust in the Lord and not be anxious?

....

2. Is worry a sin?

....

3. What area of your life is most difficult to trust God to handle?

....

P ARENT PAGE

• Distribute page to parents.

• When the groups return, read Matthew 6:25-34 and then have each group come up with as many ways as they can think of in which they saw God's care for people and the rest of His creation.

TEAM EFFORT—HIGH SCHOOL (15-20 MINUTES)

DON'T WORRY!

• Select (or ask for volunteers) five students to act out the following skit. Students could be given copies of "Don't Worry!" on pages 87 and 88 just before class, or at the previous meeting to allow them time to prepare. They can use costumes and/or props if you provide them. Let them be creative.

• Introduce the skit by saying "Jesus used stories and word pictures in this skit."

• Have two volunteers read Matthew 6:25-34 and Mark 7:7-11.

• Tell the students the following Bible background and discuss the questions.

Jesus chose twelve disciples to follow Him. These twelve left everything—jobs, homes, families—to follow Him. Along the way, Jesus gave them many lessons in God's love and care for His own.

Jesus wanted His disciples to understand that the love of God is like that of a loving father; and not just any father, but the perfect Father. Would a father on earth harm his child and give a rock instead of bread? Would he give his child something that appeared good but would bring harm, such as a white scorpion and call it an egg? A father who cares for his children would not attempt to harm them, although he sometimes does inadvertently. The perfect Father never harms His children, even unintentionally.

• Discuss the following questions:
1. How do you relate this skit to your own life?
2. Why do you think people worry? What do you know about God that will help you when you are worried or afraid?
3. How did God show His love for people in the Bible? How has He shown His love for you?
4. What can you do to thank God for His love?

IN THE WORD (25-30 MINUTES)

Do Not Worry

• Divide students into groups of three or four.
• Give each student a copy of "Do Not Worry" on pages 89 and 90 and a pen or pencil, or display the page using an overhead projector.
• Have students complete the Bible study.

AVOIDING THE ANXIETY ATTACK
Read Matthew 6:25-34.
What is the first, bold command of Jesus in this passage?

What example does Jesus use to show us God cares about our need for food?

Our need for clothes?

What do you think Jesus is trying to say to us when He compares our needs with those of the birds and flowers?

What does Matthew 6:27 tell you about God's care for you?

PUTTING YOUR TRUST IN CHRIST
According to verse 30, what is it we lack when we worry?

In your own words, write what Jesus is saying in verse 33.

What practical advice does Jesus give in verse 34?

FLYING WITH WINGS OF FAITH
Circle the following sentence completions that best describe you.
If I were a bird of the air and my heavenly Father were looking at me, I think He would see...
1. an eagle—flying strongly.
2. a chicken—running crazily.
3. a baby bird—waiting to be fed.
4. an owl—wise and silent.
5. an ostrich—unable to fly.
6. a parrot—talking, talking, talking.
7. a crow—noisy and lazy.
8. a condor—different, rare and unique.
9. a sea gull—soaring to heaven.
10. a toucan—bright and colorful.

Circle the answers that apply to you.
The things that keep me grounded and unable to fly are...
1. doubting God.
2. distrust of people.
3. a bad experience.
4. unforgiven sin.
5. laziness.
6. distractions of the world.
7. bitterness in relationships.
8. lack of support.
9. too much worry.
10. other.

Finish this sentence:
For me to fly high with faith and trust in God, I need to...

TRUSTING THE LORD
Why is it difficult for you to trust in the Lord and not be anxious?

**TRUST VERSUS
ANXIETY**

DON'T WORRY[1]

Characters: James, John, Peter, Philip, Matthew

James: (whining) We sure have to walk a long way. What happens if our sandals wear out? Where are we going to find the money to buy new ones?

John: And what about our cloaks? Each of us has only one. What happens when a cloak gets a hole in it?

Peter: Weren't you Sons of Thunder listening to the Master today? Didn't He tell us not to worry about what we would wear? Didn't He remind us that the flowers of the field don't have to shear sheep or spin wool to weave their yarn into clothes?

Philip: That's right. Even Solomon, the richest king Israel has ever known, didn't have clothing as beautiful as the way God clothes the flowers.

Peter: Right. I wish you two would listen to what the Master says instead of always worrying. Besides, if you want to worry about something, worry about food. It's getting late and we're nowhere near any town. How are we going to fill our bellies tonight?

Matthew: That's you right to the core, Peter. Always worrying about your belly. When have we ever gone hungry since being with the Master? But you still worry about food. If you're going to be like that, go back to fishing.

Peter: At least I had an honorable profession before joining Jesus. I wasn't a lousy tax gatherer, working for the Romans.

Philip: Knock it off, Peter. You may not have been a tax gatherer before you met Jesus, but you weren't the best person in the country. How many fights did you get into over nothing?

James: Besides, you aren't any better than John and me.

John: That's right. You don't listen any better than we do to what the Master says. Didn't He tell us today not to worry about food?

Philip: They've got you there, Peter. Remember what He said about birds? God doesn't let them starve. He takes care of them.

Matthew: He even talked about how much more valuable we are than those birds. He said, "Five sparrows are sold for a few pennies..."

Peter: Trust a tax collector to know the price of everything.

Matthew: Better than only knowing about scaling fish and fixing nets.

Philip: Would you two stop bickering? How do you think Jesus would feel if He heard you two? Keep it up and you'll make the Pharisees look good.

Peter: What do you mean?

Philip: Don't they say one thing and do another? That makes them hypocrites. You two are acting exactly the same way, saying Jesus is your Master and then behaving the way you do. It's disgusting. Worrying and fighting over every little thing, when the only important thing to worry about is what's going to

happen to us and our families—being separated for so long. How will everyone survive? Are we doing the right thing or not?

James : (to John) Maybe Philip needs a taste of his own medicine.

John: A little reminder of the Master's words.

Philip: What are you two going on about?

Matthew: Should we explain it to him, Peter?

Peter: (to Matthew) Sure. You do it. You're the educated man. You know bigger words.

Matthew: Anybody could explain this. Remember Jesus asking, "If a child was hungry and asked his father for a piece of bread..."

Peter: "Would that father give the child a stone that looked like bread?"

James: "And if the child asked for a piece of fish..."

John: "Would the father give the child a snake that is not to be eaten?"

Peter: "And if earthly fathers, who sin, are kind to their children..."

Matthew: "How much more kind is our Father in heaven, who knows what we need even before we ask for it."

Philip: OK, so I'm not perfect either. I guess we all need to stick close to Jesus to understand what He says and put His words into practice.

Note:

1. *The Bible Skit Book, Vol. 1* (Ventura, Calif.: Gospel Light, 1993), pp. 82-83.

TRUST VERSUS ANXIETY

IN THE WORD

DO NOT WORRY
Read Matthew 6:25-34.

Avoiding the Anxiety Attack

What is the first, bold command of Jesus in this passage?

....

....

What example does Jesus use to show us God cares about our need for food?

....

....

Our need for clothes?

....

....

What do you think Jesus is trying to say to us when He compares our needs with those of the birds and flowers?

....

....

What does Matthew 6:27 tell you about God's care for you?

....

....

Putting Your Trust in Christ
According to verse 30, what is it we lack when we worry?

....

....

In your own words, write what Jesus is saying in verse 33.

....

....

What practical advice does Jesus give in verse 34?

....

....

Flying with Wings of Faith
Circle the following sentence completions that best describe you:

If I were a bird of the air and my heavenly Father were looking at me, I think He would see...

1. an eagle—flying strongly.
2. a chicken—running crazy.
3. a baby bird—waiting to be fed.
4. an owl—wise and silent.

5. an ostrich—unable to fly.

6. a parrot—talking, talking, talking.

7. a crow—noisy and lazy.

8. a condor—different, rare and unique.

9. a sea gull—soaring to heaven.

10. a toucan—bright and colorful.

Circle the answers that apply to you.

The things that keep me grounded and unable to fly are...

1. doubting God.

2. distrust of people.

3. a bad experience.

4. unforgiven sin.

5. laziness.

6. distractions of the world.

7. bitterness in relationships.

8. lack of support.

9. too much worry.

10. other:..

Finish this sentence:

For me to fly high with faith and trust in God, I need to...

....

....

Trusting the Lord

Why is it difficult to trust in the Lord and not be anxious?

....

....

So What?

Finish the following sentence:

Since God is able to care for the needs of the flowers and birds, then He is definitely able to care for my needs in the areas of...

....

....

Things to Think About

1. **Why is it difficult to trust in the Lord and not be anxious?**

....

....

2. **Is worry a sin?**

....

....

3. **What area of your life is most difficult to trust God to handle?**

....

....

PARENT PAGE

THE FAITH FACTOR

Here are a few words on faith from three Christian leaders of the past. Read these together as a family and discuss their meanings.

"I had rather exercise faith than know the definition thereof."—Thomas à Kempis

"Faith is a redirection of our sight, a getting out of the focus of our own vision and getting God into focus."—A.W. Tozer

"True faith in its very essence rests in this—a leaning upon Christ. It will not save me to know that Christ is a Savior; but it will save me to trust Him to be my Savior."—Charles Spurgeon

What encouragement and insight can you get from these words about faith?

....

....

Read together Hebrews 11:1,6.
What is a good practical definition of faith?

....

....

....

How does faith in God play an important factor in our family's life?

....

....

....

According to verse 6, how can we please God?

....

....

....

What promises from Matthew 6:25-34 help us in our decisions to live in faith?

....

....

....

Session 7: "Trust Versus Anxiety"
Date...

JUDGING OTHERS AND OURSELVES

KEY VERSES

"'Do not judge, or you too will be judged. For in the same way you judge others, you will be judged, and with the measure you use, it will be measured to you.'" Matthew 7:1,2

BIBLICAL BASIS

Deuteronomy 1:17;
Matthew 6:2,5,16; 7:1-5;
Luke 6:37,38;
John 8:1-11;
1 Peter 2:1

THE BIG IDEA

Christians are judged by the standard they use to judge other people. Therefore, evaluate and change your own life before you judge others.

AIMS OF THIS SESSION

During this session you will guide students to:
• Examine the biblical concept of judging others;
• Discover what it is that God wants to do in their lives in relation to judging others;
• Implement a specific plan to deal with areas of their lives that they need to work on before they judge others.

WARM UP

MY DAILY ROUTINE—
Students share about their daily lives with one another.

TEAM EFFORT— JUNIOR HIGH/ MIDDLE SCHOOL

THE ENGLISH TEST—
An activity to illustrate the difficulties caused by being too quick to judge.

TEAM EFFORT— HIGH SCHOOL

A STONE REMINDER—
A discussion about how to avoid making wrong judgments.

IN THE WORD

A HEART TRANSPLANT AND EYE SURGERY—
A Bible study on judging others.

THINGS TO THINK ABOUT (OPTIONAL)

Questions to get students thinking and talking about applying Jesus' teaching on judgment of others.

PARENT PAGE

A tool to get the session into the home and allow parents and young people to discuss their family's attitude about judging others.

LEADER'S DEVOTIONAL

"Do not show partiality in judging; hear both small and great alike. Do not be afraid of any man, for judgment belongs to God" (Deuteronomy 1:17).

Isn't it amazing how the kids you'd least expect to come to the Lord are the ones that always do? As a youth worker, I can honestly say that my judgments about some teenagers are often quite offtrack. Like anyone else, I'm prone to make quick assumptions about students by their style of dress, the way they cut their hair, what color they dye it, how many body piercings they have and the number of tatoos on their arms or legs. I wish I could judge all kids fairly and justly, but when it comes right down to it, the majority of kids that I've developed good relationships with are the ones who have a lot in common with me. In fact, in a few ways, some of these students are just like *me*!

Isn't that what judging others and making faulty assumptions is all about? We want people (even students) to be just like us. If they're not, then a quick judgement is made, the person is categorized, stereotyped and filed in our mental card catalog. As the bearers of righteousness and truth, we "know" what's right and wrong. Our perception, intuition and telescopic eyesight is so good that we are experts at discovering the teeny, tiny specks of dust in the eyes of others. We are masters at whacking others with our hypocritical judgement planks. There's got to be a better way.

I am so glad that Jesus, the one and only Judge, told us not to judge others. He knew we had an incredible capacity to avoid taking responsibility for our own actions, attitudes and personal weaknesses. How easy it is to judge someone else instead of ourselves! My hope for you in this lesson is that you and your students will become more like Christ—people of grace and humility. I'm sure you've already seen a number of teenagers whose lives have been changed in your youth ministry because of being unconditionallly accepted and cared for. They weren't judged. They were loved. Be like Jesus: look beyond the outside appearances and actions. Judge not lest you be judged. Or better yet, just love them. (Written by Joey O'Connor.)

"Examine the contents, not the bottle."
—The Talmud

JUDGING OTHERS AND OURSELVES

KEY VERSES

"Do not judge, or you too will be judged. For in the same way you judge others, you will be judged, and with the measure you use, it will be measured to you.'" Matthew 7:1,2

BIBLICAL BASIS

Deuteronomy 1:17; Matthew 6:2,5,16; 7:1-5; Luke 6:37,38; John 8:1-11; 1 Peter 2:1

THE BIG IDEA

Christians are judged by the standard they use to judge other people. Therefore, evaluate and change your own life before you judge others.

WARM UP (5-10 MINUTES)

My Daily Routine

• Give each student a copy of "My Daily Routine" on page 97 and a pen or pencil, or display a copy using an overhead projector.
• Divide students into groups of three or four.
• Have students complete the page and share their answers with others in their group.

Complete the sentences and share your answers with your group.

1. I usually wake up at...
2. I start the day by...
3. For breakfast, I usually eat...
4. My most creative time in the day is...
5. My favorite time of the day is...
6. The people I enjoy being around most are...
7. My favorite thing to do is...
8. I usually get to bed around...

---- Fold ----

Is there anyone you need to talk to? If so, who?

How will this new understanding influence your future behavior? List a change you might experience in each of the following areas:

Relationship with Christ

Family

School

Sports/Clubs

Friends

Social Life

Dating Life

Other

TIME FOR EYE SURGERY—MATTHEW 7:3-5

Read Matthew 7:3-5.

"This might hurt a little." These are famous last words, but true, especially when it comes to adjusting our own words and actions. Are there any boards sticking out of your eyes? If so, don't worry, you are human.

What is the problem with the person Jesus spoke of in Matthew 7:3-5?

How does a person do what Jesus commands in verse 5?

SO WHAT?

In the space below write out the areas of your life that need "eye surgery." If you need help "removing the plank," write out the name of a person who might be able to help you.

THINGS TO THINK ABOUT (OPTIONAL)

• Use the questions on page 100 after or as a part of "In the Word."

1. Why is judging other people hypocritical according to Jesus?

2. Which people in your life receive most of your criticism? Why?

3. Why is "self-judgment" painful?

PARENT PAGE

• Distribute page to parents.

THE ENGLISH TEST

Below is a fun way to show students how we often make judgments too hastily.

• Give each student a copy of "The English Test" on page 97 and a pen or pencil.

• Prepare a transparency, or copy the paragraph on poster board with the correct punctuation, to show them the proper form.

• Have each person make the corrections as instructed.

• When they are finished, read and discuss Matthew 7:1-5.

Here is the way it should be corrected:

He is a young man, yet experienced. In vice and wickedness, he is never found. In opposing the works of iniquity, he takes delight. In the downfall of his neighbors, he never rejoices. In the prosperity of his fellow-creatures, he is always ready to assist. In destroying the peace of society, he takes no pleasure. In serving the Lord, he is uncommonly diligent. In sowing discord among his friends and acquaintances, he takes no pride. In laboring to promote the cause of Christianity, he has not been negligent. In endeavoring to tear down the church, he makes no effort. To subdue his evil passions, he strives hard. To build up Satan's kingdom, he lends no aid. To the support of the gospel among the heathen, he contributes largely. To Heaven he must go, where he will receive his just reward. To the devil he will never go.

TEAM EFFORT—HIGH SCHOOL (15-20 MINUTES)

A STONE REMINDER

• Give each person a stone or rock.

• Read John 8:1-11 aloud.

• Discuss the following questions while holding the stone/rock:

What sin was this woman caught in?

Did the people have the right to judge the woman caught in adultery? Why or why not?

How did Jesus judge her properly?

What judgment sins do we make? (Brainstorm things like gossip, others' lifestyle choices, spirituality.)

Encourage the students to take the stone/rock home with them and ask themselves these two questions when they are tempted to judge others:

1. Am I without sin?

2. Am I qualified to take the stone and throw it at this person?

Option: Distribute permanent markers and have the students write "Am I without sin?" on the stone or rock.

- Fold -

IN THE WORD (25-30 MINUTES)

A HEART TRANSPLANT AND EYE SURGERY

• Divide students into groups of three or four.

• Give each student a copy of "A Heart Transplant and Eye Surgery" on pages 98, 99 and 100 and a pen or pencil, or display the page using an overhead projector.

• Have students complete the Bible study.

Read Matthew 7:1-5.

HERE COMES THE JUDGE

According to the words of Jesus, what happens to a judgmental person?

Read Matthew 7:1-5.

Why do you think Jesus includes a teaching on judging others in the context of the Sermon on the Mount?

Why do you think Jesus can say something like this after being so critical of the Jewish leaders? [See Matthew 6:2,5,16.]

According to Jesus, who is most responsible for the condemnation we receive?

How does Luke sum up the teaching in verse 38?

Read Luke 6:37,38. What additional words of Jesus does Luke include in this teaching?

BE CAREFUL WHAT YOU SAY—MATTHEW 7:1,2

Read Matthew 7:1,2.

The Miranda Act, a rights protection law, is known by many of us because of the TV shows that use it in police scenes.

Does this sound familiar?

You have the absolute right to remain silent. Anything you say can and will be used as evidence against you in a court of law. You have the right to consult with an attorney, to be represented by an attorney, to have an attorney present before any questions are asked and during any time that questions are asked. If you cannot afford an attorney, one will be appointed by the court, free of charge, to represent you before any questioning if you desire.

Now imagine that you are in a spiritual court.

How do you feel knowing that your speech and actions will be reviewed at your spiritual hearing?

a. I'm in trouble now.

b. I hope there wasn't a video camera near me the last few days.

c. I think it is time to ask for forgiveness.

d. Yipes!

e. I think I'm safe.

f. Thank God for forgiveness.

If you take the words Jesus spoke in Matthew 7:1-5 seriously, what steps will you need to take to put His words into action?

JUDGING OTHERS AND OURSELVES

WARM UP

MY DAILY ROUTINE

Complete the sentences and share your answers with your group.

1. I usually wake up at...
2. I start the day by...
3. For breakfast, I usually eat...
4. My most creative time in the day is...
5. My favorite time of the day is...
6. The people I enjoy being around most are...
7. My favorite thing to do is...
8. I usually get to bed around...

TEAM EFFORT

THE ENGLISH TEST[1]

Make this paragraph into sentences using capitals at the beginning, periods at the end of sentences, and commas, etc. where needed. Once begun, **do not go back** and try to correct.

> He is a young man yet experienced in vice and wickedness he is never found in opposing the works of iniquity he takes delight in the downfall of his neighbors he never rejoices in the prosperity of his fellow-creatures he is always ready to assist in destroying the peace of society he takes no pleasure in serving the Lord he is uncommonly diligent in sowing discord among his friends and acquaintances he takes no pride in laboring to promote the cause of Christianity he has not been negligent in endeavoring to tear down the church he makes no effort to subdue his evil passions he strives hard to build up Satan's kingdom he lends no aid to the support of the gospel among heathen he contributes largely to the devil he will never go to Heaven he must go where he will receive his just reward.

Note:

1. *Ideas Number 17-20* (El Cajon, Calif.: Youth Specialties, 1981), pp. 83-84.

IN THE WORD

A HEART TRANSPLANT AND EYE SURGERY
Read Matthew 7:1-5.
Here Comes the Judge

According to the words of Jesus, what happens to a judgmental person?

....

....

Read Luke 6:37,38. What additional words of Jesus does Luke include in this teaching?

....

....

How does Luke sum up the teaching in verse 38?

....

....

According to Jesus, who is most responsible for the condemnation we receive?

....

....

Why do you think Jesus includes a teaching on judging others in the context of the Sermon on the Mount?

....

....

Why do you think Jesus can say something like this after being so critical of the Jewish leaders? (See Matthew 6:2,5,16.)

....

....

Be Careful What You Say—Matthew 7:1,2
Read Matthew 7:1,2.

The Miranda Act, a rights protection law, is known by many of us because of the TV shows that use it in police scenes. Does this sound familiar?

> You have the absolute right to remain silent. Anything you say can and will be used as evidence against you in a court of law. You have the right to consult with an attorney, to be represented by an attorney, to have an attorney present before any questions are asked and during any time that questions are asked. If you cannot afford an attorney, one will be appointed by the court, free of charge, to represent you before any questioning if you desire.

Now imagine that you are in a spiritual court.

How do you feel knowing that your speech and actions will be reviewed at your spiritual hearing?

    a. I'm in trouble now.

    b. I hope there wasn't a video camera near me the last few days.

    c. I think it is time to ask for forgiveness.

IN THE WORD

JUDGING OTHERS AND OURSELVES

d. Yipes!
e. I think I'm safe.
f. Thank God for forgiveness.

If you take the words Jesus spoke in Matthew 7:1-5 seriously, what steps will you need to take to put His words into action?

....

....

Is there anyone you need to talk to? If so, who?

....

How will this new understanding influence your future behavior? List a change you might experience in each of the following areas:

Relationship with Christ ....

....

Family ....

....

School ....

....

Sports/Clubs ....

....

Friends ....

....

Social Life ....

....

Dating Life ....

....

Other ....

....

Time for Eye Surgery—Matthew 7:3-5

Read Matthew 7:3-5.

"This might hurt a little." These are famous last words, but true, especially when it comes to adjusting our own words and actions. Are there any boards sticking out of your eyes? If so, don't worry, you are human.

What is the problem with the person Jesus spoke of in Matthew 7:3-5?

....

....

....

How does a person do what Jesus commands in verse 5?

....

....

So What?

In the space below write out the areas of your life that need "eye surgery." If you need help "removing the plank," write out the name of a person who might be able to help you.

....

....

Things to Think About

1. Why is judging other people hypocritical according to Jesus?

....

....

2. Which people in your life receive most of your criticism? Why?

....

....

3. Why is "self-judgment" painful?

....

....

PARENT PAGE

JUDGMENTAL OR AFFIRMING?

Here's some great advice from the apostle Peter:

"So get rid of your feelings of hatred. Don't just pretend to be good! Be done with dishonesty and jealousy and talking about others behind their backs" (1 Peter 2:1, *TLB*).

As a family, give yourself a grade for talking behind others' backs:

.... **A** We seldom, if ever, do it.

.... **B** Above the average—not much of a problem.

.... **C** Sometimes we do and sometimes we don't.

.... **D** Oops! This is a big problem in our family.

.... **F** We need major work in this area.

What kind of impact do you have on people? Are you a person of affirmation or are you a judgmental, critical person?
Place a mark on the line below and tell your family why you placed it where you did. Do they agree?

....

Affirming/Encouraging   **Critical/Judgmental**

A famous author once said, "For every one critical statement it takes nine affirming statements to make up for the one critical comment."
Is our family more critical/judgmental, or more affirming to each other?

....

What can we all do to be more affirming and encouraging?

....

....

When you leave this world, what would you like people to say about you?

....

....

Session 8: "Judging Others and Ourselves"
Date..

Unit III

DECISIONS

LEADER'S PEP TALK

Here's a typical Jim and Cathy Burns date: We give instructions to the baby sitter, kiss the girls, check the wallet for money, pick up the car keys, give more instructions to the baby sitter, kiss the girls again, get in the car, pull out of the driveway and drive down the street.

I then ask Cathy, "Where do you want to eat?"

"Oh, I really don't care. Where do *you* want to eat?"

"It doesn't matter."

"Well, what kind of food do you want?"

"How about Mexican food?"

"Not Mexican."

"Do you feel like Italian? Fish? Burgers? How about Chinese food?"

"No, I don't think so."

"I know, let's go get a salad."

"I don't want a salad."

"Well, what do you want?"

"I don't care."

Sometimes we have to stop the car and *decide to decide*.

We sound a little like today's youth. The problem with this generation of students is not that they make *dumb* decisions, but that they don't make *enough* decisions. Such failure leads many wonderful, incredible people into big trouble.

This last section is really about decisions. You will teach your students how to make wise decisions—decisions they will live with for a lifetime.

Thanks for helping them "decide to decide" to put their trust in the Lord. I can't think of a more important job than what you are doing—helping kids make positive, eternal decisions.

And God smiled.

THE POWER OF PRAYER

Key Verses

"'Ask and it will be given to you; seek and you will find; knock and the door will be opened to you. For everyone who asks receives; he who seeks finds; and to him who knocks, the door will be opened.

'Which of you, if his son asks for bread, will give him a stone? Or if he asks for a fish, will give him a snake? If you, then, though you are evil, know how to give good gifts to your children, how much more will your Father in heaven give good gifts to those who ask him!'"
Matthew 7:7-11

Biblical Basis
1 Samuel 1:10,11,20;
Matthew 7:7-12; 21:22;
Luke 11:5-10;
Hebrews 11:1;
James 5:16;
1 John 5:14,15

The Big Idea
The Lord hears our prayers and responds to our needs.

Aims of This Session
During this session you will guide students to:
- Examine the nature of prayer and the gifts of the Father;
- Discover the meaning of the "Golden Rule";
- Implement how to practically apply this Scripture to their lives.

Warm Up
The World's Worst Joke Contest—
Students judge each other's joke entries.

Team Effort—Junior High/Middle School
Removing the Roadblocks to Prayer
Students consider how to improve their prayer lives.

Team Effort—High School
Let's Pray—
Students spend time in prayer.

In the Word
Ask, Seek, Knock—
A Bible study on discovering the nature of prayer.

Things to Think About (Optional)
Questions to get students thinking and talking about their prayer lives.

Parent Page
A tool to get the session into the home and allow parents and young people to discuss how to experience the joy of prayer.

Decisions

LEADER'S DEVOTIONAL

"Therefore confess your sins to each other and pray for each other so that you may be healed. The prayer of a righteous man is powerful and effective" (James 5:16).

In the early days of our youth ministry, I think we spent more time in prayer than we did after our group grew to a considerable size. That's not something I'm very proud of, but it's the truth. I can remember meeting with a couple of our volunteer staff members and going down the roster of each student who had signed up for winter or summer camp. I remember that we prayed for each student specifically, by name.

As the ministry grew, we became busier and busier. There were more students signing up at the last minute, more cabin assignments to make, transportation details to finalize and more volunteer staff meetings. We became better at running camps, but our prayers for the Holy Spirit to work in students' lives actually decreased. We became less dependent on God and more dependent on ourselves. Without prayer, there wasn't the passion for God like there used to be.

You've heard the old saying, "If the devil doesn't make you sin, he'll make you busy." The devil would love for us not to pray. What I experienced in our youth ministry wasn't unusual for most churches, youth ministries or Christians. It wasn't that prayer was no longer important to us. We still prayed. Our problem with prayer was a question of priorities and where prayer fell on our list of things to do.

When we pray, our primary purpose isn't to ask or receive. The purpose of prayer is to be with God: to sit and wait and to listen. Just like Jesus went to a solitary place early in the morning to be with and pray to His Father, we are to increase our desire for meeting with and praying to the Lord. Hopefully, the story of our youth ministry will change some things about the priority of prayer in your youth ministry (or maybe we can learn something from you!). This lesson is a great place to talk about the priority of prayer in your youth ministry and the incredible difference that your meeting with God can make in each of your student's lives. As you prepare this lesson, my prayers are with you. (Written by Joey O'Connor.)

"Prayer does not change God, but changes him who prays."
—Soren Kierkegaard

THE POWER OF PRAYER

KEY VERSES

"Ask and it will be given to you; seek and you will find; knock and the door will be opened to you. For everyone who asks receives; he who seeks finds; and to him who knocks, the door will be opened.

"Which of you, if his son asks for bread, will give him a stone? Or if he asks for a fish, will give him a snake? If you, then, though you are evil, know how to give good gifts to your children, how much more will your Father in heaven give good gifts to those who ask him!" Matthew 7:7-11

BIBLICAL BASIS

1 Samuel 1:10,11,20; Matthew 7:7-12; 21:22; Luke 11:5-10; Hebrews 11:1; James 5:16; 1 John 5:14,15

THE BIG IDEA

The Lord hears our prayers and responds to our needs.

WARM UP (5-10 MINUTES)

THE WORLD'S WORST JOKE CONTEST

• The idea behind this event is to have your students come up with "the world's worst joke."

• Give the students a chance to "enter" a joke and have the other students decide who told the worst joke. You could award silly prizes to the "winners."

TEAM EFFORT—JUNIOR HIGH/

MIDDLE SCHOOL (15-20 MINUTES)

REMOVING THE ROADBLOCKS TO PRAYER

• Give each student a copy of "Removing the Roadblocks to Prayer" on page 109 and a pen or pencil.

• Have students complete the page.

---- Fold ----

SO WHAT?

How can you practically apply this message on prayer to your life? (Be as specific as possible.)

THINGS TO THINK ABOUT (OPTIONAL)

• Use the questions on page 112 after or as a part of "In the Word."

1. What has been the biggest help to your prayer life?

2. How is Matthew 7:7-12 such a positive illustration of God's love?

3. What is the greatest need you have right now and want to give to God in prayer?

PARENT PAGE

• Distribute page to parents.

- Divide students into pairs and have them share their responses and then spend a moment praying for each other.

Finish this sentence: The biggest roadblock(s) in my prayer life is (are)...

Which of these ingredients would best help your prayer life? Circle the most appropriate response.
1. Praying on a regular basis.
2. Believing God will answer.
3. Praying with others.
4. Seeing more results from my prayers.
5. Getting over the embarrassment of praying with others.
6. Keeping track of my prayers in a journal.
7. Finding creative ideas for prayer.
8. Studying the Bible and other books about prayer.
9. Scheduling time in my day to pray.
10. Using Scripture to help me pray.

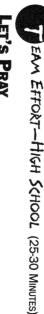

TEAM EFFORT—HIGH SCHOOL (25-30 MINUTES)

LET'S PRAY

- Give students a copy of "Let's Pray" on page 110 and a pen or pencil.
- Have someone read the Scripture aloud.
- Have students pair up and take a moment or two to jot down specific requests beside each of the suggestions below. Then have students pray with their partners.

You can talk about prayer. You can study the concept and essentials of prayer. You can debate the various philosophies about prayer, but if you don't pray, you will never experience the power of prayer. Read Matthew 7:7-12. Then take several minutes to pray. Use this format if you like.

Lord, we pray for...
1. our families.
2. our school.
3. sharing of our faith.
4. missions.
5. spiritual integrity.
6. the church.
7. strength to follow Christ.

 ### IN THE WORD (25-30 MINUTES)

ASK, SEEK, KNOCK

- Divide students into groups of three or four.
- Give each student a copy of "Ask, Seek, Knock" on pages 111 and 112 and a pen or pencil, or display the page using an overhead projector.
- Have students complete the Bible study.

— Fold —

Read Matthew 7:7-12.

DISCOVERING THE NATURE OF PRAYER—MATTHEW 7:7,8
What kind of invitation do we receive in verses 7 and 8?

What do you think keeps most believers from asking, seeking and knocking more often?

Read the parable in Luke 11:5-10. What characteristics of the friend at the door caused the man in the house to open the door?

It is important to note that the words ask, seek and knock are all written in the future present tense, which is best translated: keep on asking, keep on seeking and keep on knocking. How does this knowledge help you understand verses 7 and 8?

THE GOOD GIFTS OF THE FATHER—MATTHEW 7:9-11
Why do you think Jesus compared the gifts of an earthly father with the response of our Heavenly Father?

Prayer was instrumental in the rise of Israel in Old Testament times. God chose to use the prayer of Hannah, a humble woman, to help bring about Israel's greatness. Read Hannah's prayer (see 1 Samuel 1:10,11). What are some of the features of her prayer?

What gift did Hannah receive from the Lord? (See 1 Samuel 1:20.)

Samuel grew to be a great prophet and leader of Israel. It was Samuel who anointed David when God chose David to be king of Israel.
How do the following verses influence your attitude about prayer?
Matthew 21:22

Hebrews 11:1

1 John 5:14,15

THE GOLDEN RULE—MATTHEW 7:12
What makes Matthew 7:12 such an important statement about how we should treat others?

What do you think Jesus meant when He said "For this sums up the law and the Prophets"?

THE POWER OF PRAYER

 EAM EFFORT

REMOVING THE ROADBLOCKS TO PRAYER

Finish this sentence: The biggest roadblock(s) in my prayer life is (are)...

....

....

Which of these ingredients would best help your prayer life? Circle the most appropriate response.

1. Praying on a regular basis.

2. Believing God will answer.

3. Praying with others.

4. Seeing more results from my prayers.

5. Getting over the embarrassment of praying with others.

6. Keeping track of my prayers in a journal.

7. Finding creative ideas for prayer.

8. Studying the Bible and other books about prayer.

9. Scheduling time in my day to pray.

10. Using Scripture to help me pray.

TEAM EFFORT

LET'S PRAY

You can talk about prayer. You can study the concept and essentials of prayer. You can debate the various philosophies about prayer, but if you don't pray, you will never experience the power of prayer.

Read Matthew 7:7-12. Then take several minutes to pray. Use this format if you like.

Lord, we pray for...

1. our families.

2. our school.

3. sharing of our faith.

4. missions.

5. spiritual integrity.

6. the church.

7. strength to follow Christ.

THE POWER OF PRAYER

IN THE WORD

ASK, SEEK, KNOCK
Read Matthew 7:7-12.

Discovering the Nature of Prayer—Matthew 7:7,8
What kind of invitation do we receive in verses 7 and 8?

....

....

What do you think keeps most believers from asking, seeking and knocking more often?

....

....

Read the parable in Luke 11:5-10. What characteristics of the friend at the door caused the man in the house to open the door?

....

....

It is important to note that the words ask, seek and knock are all written in the future present tense, which is best translated: keep on asking, keep on seeking and keep on knocking. How does this knowledge help you understand verses 7 and 8?

....

....

The Good Gifts of the Father—Matthew 7:9-11
Why do you think Jesus compared the gifts of an earthly father with the response of our Heavenly Father?

....

....

Prayer was instrumental in the rise of Israel in Old Testament times. God chose to use the prayer of Hannah, a humble woman, to help bring about Israel's greatness.

Read Hannah's prayer (see 1 Samuel 1:10,11). What are some of the features of her prayer?

....

....

What gift did Hannah receive from the Lord? (See 1 Samuel 1:20.)

....

....

Samuel grew to be a great prophet and leader of Israel. It was Samuel who anointed David when God chose David to be king of Israel.

How do the following verses influence your attitude about prayer?

Matthew 21:22 ....

....

Hebrews 11:1 ....

....

1 John 5:14,15 ....

....

The Golden Rule—Matthew 7:12
What makes Matthew 7:12 such an important statement about how we should treat others?

....

....

What do you think Jesus meant when He said "For this sums up the Law and the Prophets"?

....

....

So What?
How can you practically apply this message to your life? (Be as specific as possible.)

....

....

THINGS TO THINK ABOUT

1. What has been the biggest help to your prayer life?

....

....

2. How is Matthew 7:7-12 such a positive illustration of God's love?

....

....

3. What is the greatest need you have right now and want to give to God in prayer?

....

....

DECISIONS

THE POWER OF
PRAYER

PARENT PAGE

EXPERIENCING THE JOY OF PRAYER

Read Matthew 7:7-12. In this section of Scripture, Jesus enlarges our prayer life by discussing the true nature of God's care as compared to an earthly father. An important ingredient for prayer is the realization that God is infinite—not subject to any limitations in space, time, knowledge or power.

Complete the following sentence with several different words describing God. (Examples: alive, caring, powerful, etc.)

The God to whom I pray is... ....

....

We experience the joy of prayer when we have a proper understanding of what prayer is and what prayer is not.

Take a few moments to complete the following statements with several examples.

Prayer is not... ....

....

Prayer is... ....

....

Where is the best place for you to pray?

....

....

When is the best time for you to pray?

....

....

What is the best method for your prayer time?

....

Here is what Mother Teresa of Calcutta, India said about prayer:

> Love to pray. Feel often during the day the need for prayer, and take trouble to pray. Prayer enlarges the heart until it is capable of containing God's gift of Himself. Ask and seek, and your heart will grow big enough to receive Him and keep Him as your own.[1]

Now read Matthew 7:7-12 again with Mother Teresa's powerful words on your mind. Then, as a family, write out a prayer request list for your concerned Heavenly Father to see and hear.

....

....

Note:

1. From Mother Teresa, *A Gift for God*, quoted by Reuben P. Job and Norman Shawchuck in *A Guide to Prayer* (Nashville: The Upper Room, 1983), pp. 233-234.

Session 9: "The Power of Prayer"
Date ....

DECISIONS AND THE NARROW GATE

K EY VERSES

"'Enter through the narrow gate. For wide is the gate and broad is the road that leads to destruction, and many enter through it. But small is the gate and narrow the road that leads to life, and only a few find it.'" Matthew 7:13,14

B IBLICAL BASIS

Deuteronomy 30:15-20;
Matthew 7:13,14;
John 10:9,10;
John 14:1-6

T HE BIG IDEA

Choosing to live for Christ may at times be costly, but that decision leads to eternal and abundant life.

A IMS OF THIS SESSION

During this session you will guide students to:
• Examine the need to make decisions based on God's principles;
• Discover which decisions about their faith and life require that they take the narrow path;

• Implement a plan to make the right decisions and then follow through on those decisions.

W ARM UP

THE MATCH GAME—
A fun activity matching puns.

T EAM EFFORT— JUNIOR HIGH/ MIDDLE SCHOOL

LET'S TALK—
Students consider the advice to give to others in various decision-making situations.

T EAM EFFORT— HIGH SCHOOL

COUNTING THE COST—
Students consider what it means to chose God's way.

I N THE WORD

CHOOSING THE NARROW GATE—
A Bible study on making the decisions needed to live a Christlike life.

T HINGS TO THINK ABOUT (OPTIONAL)

Questions to get students thinking and talking about making God-centered decisions.

P ARENT PAGE

A tool to get the session into the home and allow parents and young people to discuss what is and is not important in life.

DECISIONS

LEADER'S DEVOTIONAL

"This day I call heaven and earth as witnesses against you that I have set before you life and death, blessings and curses. Now choose life, so that you and your children may live and that you may love the LORD your God, listen to his voice, and hold fast to him" (Deuteronomy 30:19,20).

Without a doubt, helping young people to make good decisions is at the heart of youth ministry. Why? Because it is from every decision a young person makes that their character is either shaped to be like Christ's, or it's conformed to the pattern of this world. From these choices teenagers will shape the rest of their lives: they will either walk with God or not, follow the crowd or not, choose to be sexually active or not, experiment with drugs or not and develop healthy, positive disciplines or not. The decisions teenagers make today will affect who they become tomorrow.

Your decision to be involved in the lives of young people is an important life-changing decision that will make a difference for all eternity. You are making a critical difference in kids' lives. You probably don't feel that way when it's 11 P.M. and you're still picking up popcorn after a crazy youth event. You probably don't feel like you're making much of a difference when kids grumble, complain and never say a word of thanks.

Even as you sit down to prepare this Bible study, most students will never realize the thought, time and energy you've spent preparing something as meaningful as God's word for them to dig into. You are doing the unnoticed highly important kingdom work of helping kids enter through the narrow gate.

I hope that this week, maybe even today, God will encourage you in a very special way. My prayer is that God will confirm your ministry to teenagers. I also pray that He will give you the vision and faith to hang in there when you feel like giving up. If you ever find yourself wondering what you're doing in youth ministry, remember that your decision to love and be with kids will affect them for the rest of their lives. (Written by Joey O'Connor.)

> "Decision is a sharp knife that cuts clean and straight; indecision is a dull one that hacks and tears and leaves ragged edges behind it."—Gordon Graham

DECISIONS AND THE NARROW GATE

EY VERSES

"Enter through the narrow gate. For wide is the gate and broad is the road that leads to destruction, and many enter through it. But small is the gate and narrow the road that leads to life, and only a few find it." Matthew 7:13,14

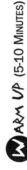IBLICAL BASIS

Deuteronomy 30:15-20; Matthew 7:13,14; John 10:9.10; John 14:1-6

THE BIG IDEA

Choosing to live for Christ may at times be costly, but that decision leads to eternal and abundant life.

WARM UP (5-10 MINUTES)

THE MATCH GAME

• Before the session gather the following items and display them on a table or scatter them around the room: the letter "O" on a card, a kernel of corn, a rubber band, a ruler, a pillow, a spoon, the letter "R," two banana peels, an old ribbon bow, a pair of scissors, a dictionary, tacks on tea bags, a mirror, an umbrella, an alarm clock, a pitcher, a match, a nail, shoe polish, rice, a hot dog and dirt.

• Give each student a copy of "The Match Game" on page 119 and a pen or pencil.

• The first student to complete the list is the winner.

• Option: Divide students into pairs or small groups and make it a race to see which team makes the most matches or finishes first.

• Answers: 1. Donut and the letter "O" on a card 2. The colonel and a kernel of corn 3. A famous band and a rubber band 4. It's a foot and a ruler 5. Headquarters and a pillow 6. A stirring event and a spoon 7. The end of winter and the letter "R" 8. A pair of slippers and two banana peels 9. An old beau of mine and an old ribbon bow 10. The peacemaker and a pair of scissors 11. Where love is found and a dictionary 12. Cause of a revolution and tacks on tea bags 13. A place for reflection and a mirror 14. The reigning favorite and an umbrella 15. A morning caller and an alarm clock 16. Seen at the ball game and a pitcher 17. Fire when ready and a match 18. Drive through the wood and a nail 19. Bound to shine and shoe polish 20. Life in China and rice 21. Top dog and a hot dog 22. My native land and dirt

— — — — — — — — — — — — — — — — Fold — — — — — — — — — — — — — — — — —

Read Deuteronomy 30:15-20. What options are listed for the Israelites?

What final command does Moses give in verse 19?

SO WHAT?

Decide to Live, Don't Live to Decide.

Many people are procrastinators when it comes to making decisions. Some people have allowed their procrastination to cause them to take the "wide road that leads to destruction." Remember, not deciding to live for Jesus is a decision!

Complete these sentences:

The biggest decisions weighing on my shoulders are...

I would make better decisions if I would...

I am glad to be alive because...

Read the following statement, then rate yourself from one to ten (ten being highest).
When it comes to discipline, saying "no" to second best for the sake of having the best, I rate myself as a ....

Circle three of your responses to the following question:
The areas of my life that are most difficult to discipline are...

eating habits	speech	sleep patterns
study habits	handling money	relationships
sexuality	church attendance	thoughts
anger/moods	humor	criticism of others
prayer life	exercise	sarcastic tongue
habit of backbiting	other:	

THINGS TO THINK ABOUT (OPTIONAL)

• Use the questions on page 124 after or as a part of "In the Word."

1. What are roadblocks to making good decisions?

2. If you knew your life would be shortened, what would you do differently?

3. What is one decision you need to give to Christ?

PARENT PAGE

• Distribute page to parents.

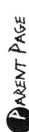

TEAM EFFORT—JUNIOR HIGH/MIDDLE SCHOOL (15-20 MINUTES)

LET'S TALK

- Divide students into groups of three or four.
- Give each student a copy of "Let's Talk" on page 120, or display the page using an overhead projector.
- Have students discuss the answers they would give.
- If time is short, assign one or two questions to each group.

Jim Burns writes a column to almost half a million teenagers a month for *Campus Life* magazine entitled "Let's Talk." You can write to him at:

Jim Burns	or
Campus Life	Jim Burns
465 Gundersen Drive	*Let's Talk*
Carol Stream, IL 60187	CLedit@aol.com

TEAM EFFORT—HIGH SCHOOL (15-20 MINUTES)

COUNTING THE COST

- Give each student a copy of "Counting the Cost" on page 121 and a pen or pencil.

Read Matthew 7:13,14. Choosing the narrow or wide path in life does require a cost.

What is the cost of the narrow way?

....

What is the cost of the wide way?

....

What can you see as the cost for the wide way?

....

What has it cost you to follow Christ?

....

What potential costs might be waiting for you to sacrifice for Christ?

....

Circle two of the following sentence completions that describe you.
I think the majority of my decisions end up...

1. being on the right track.
2. in a heap of trouble.
3. being wise and worthwhile.
4. turning out for the better eventually.
5. teaching me about failure.
6. returning to haunt me.
7. never being decided.

---

8. being decided by others.

Here's a story worth thinking about:

One morning a vulture was hungry. While flying over the river, he saw a dead animal's carcass floating down the river on a piece of ice. The vulture landed on the ice and began to gorge himself with this delightful meal. He looked up to take a breath of air and noticed that he was 100 yards from a waterfall. But instead of flying away, he kept eating, though keeping his eye on the waterfall. At 25 yards he decided to take one last bite. Then at 10 yards he took one last mouthful. With only a few feet to go before the falls he tried to fly, but his feet were now frozen to the ice, and he tumbled to his death over the falls.

What important message does this story teach us about making decisions?

....

IN THE WORD (25-30 MINUTES)

CHOOSING THE NARROW GATE

- Divide students into groups of three or four.
- Give each student a copy of "Choosing the Narrow Gate" on pages 122 and 123 and a pen or pencil, or display the page using an overhead projector.
- Have students complete the Bible study.

Read Matthew 7:13,14.

....

What choice does Jesus command before He even describes the options?

....

What makes the wide gate so popular?

....

Read John 10:9,10. In what position does Jesus place Himself?

....

What do you think the result of the wide gate, *destruction*, looks like?

....

What is the result of going through Jesus' gate?

....

Read Matthew 7:14 and John 10:10. What does Jesus mean by having life "to the full"?

....

THE ROAD LESS TRAVELED

Read John 14:1-6. "Where are we going? I don't know, do you? Who's going to lead the expedition?" You can hear the words of Thomas as he asks Jesus for directions (see v. 5).

Why do you think so few people choose the narrow gate?

....

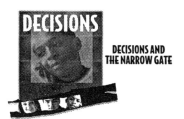

DECISIONS AND
THE NARROW GATE

WARM UP

THE MATCH GAME[1]

Match each of the following words to the displayed items. Write the name of the matching item next to the word it matches on the list.

1. Donut ....

2. The colonel ....

3. A famous band ....

4. It's a foot. ....

5. Headquarters ....

6. A stirring event ....

7. The end of winter ....

8. A pair of slippers ....

9. An old beau of mine ....

10. The peacemaker ....

11. Where love is found ....

12. Cause of a revolution ....

13. A place for reflection ....

14. The reigning favorite ....

15. A morning caller ....

16. Seen at the ball game ....

17. Fire when ready ....

18. Drive through the wood ....

19. Bound to shine ....

20. Life in China ....

21. Top dog ....

22. My native land ....

Note:

1. Adapted from Lyman Coleman, *Youth Ministry Encyclopedia* (Littleton, Colo.: Serendipity House, 1985), p. 43.

LET'S TALK

Jim Burns writes a column to almost half a million teenagers a month for *Campus Life* magazine entitled "Let's Talk." You can write him at:

Jim Burns	or	Jim Burns
Let's Talk		Let's Talk
Campus Life		CLedit@aol.com
465 Gunderson Drive		
Carol Stream, IL 60187		

Here are a few questions he has received from readers asking for help in making a decision. As a group, come up with answers for the questions. Be prepared to share your answers with the whole group.

Every time someone asks me to take on a special project (like in our youth group) I say "yes." The problem is, the more I say "yes," the more stressed out I get. I think if I said "no," I'd feel like a failure. Please tell me how I can learn to say "no" and not feel guilty for it.

Not long ago I found out a close Christian friend of mine is gay. Even though he has rejected Christian values, I decided to stand by him and try to help him. But my family (and other friends) want me to dump him. I feel like I'm caught in a tug of war. What should I do?

When I'm at youth group, everything seems great. I get along with people and I'm a positive influence on them. But when I get to school, I'm totally different. I yell at people and I'm always upset with someone. I also swear a lot (and here I am wearing a Christian T-shirt that says, "God's last name is not damn it!") I know I'm a total hypocrite but I don't know what to do about it.

I think I have an attitude problem. Sometimes I just choose to get mad. I don't know why, but I do. When I get mad I usually take it out on my parents. Afterwards I feel terrible. Sometimes I apologize. Sometimes I don't. Could you please help me figure out why I get mad so easily and how I can stop doing it?

I have a friend who is a non-Christian. We haven't been getting along very well and I would like to end the friendship. But since she is not a Christian, I feel obligated to stick with her and try to bring her to God. Is this a valid reason to continue the friendship?

I have this good friend who has started to drink and is getting involved with his girl-friend sexually. He is a Christian and knows where I stand. We've talked often about it. I find myself getting very upset with him because he doesn't seem to want to change. I have often heard we are supposed to "love the sinner and hate the sin," but could you give me some advice on how that's done? What should I do about my friend?

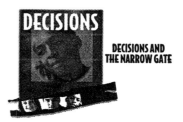

DECISIONS AND THE NARROW GATE

TEAM EFFORT

COUNTING THE COST

Read Matthew 7:13,14. Choosing the narrow or wide path in life does require a cost.

What is the cost of the narrow way?

....

....

What can you see as the cost for the wide way?

....

....

What has it cost you to follow Christ?

....

....

What potential costs might be waiting for you to sacrifice for Christ?

....

....

Circle two of the following sentence completions that describe you:

I think the majority of my decisions end up...
1. **being on the right track.**
2. **in a heap of trouble.**
3. **being wise and worthwhile.**
4. **turning out for the better eventually.**
5. **teaching me about failure.**
6. **returning to haunt me.**
7. **never being decided.**
8. **being decided by others.**

Here's a story worth thinking about:

One morning a vulture was hungry. While flying over the river, he saw a dead animal's carcass floating down the river on a piece of ice. The vulture landed on the ice and began to gorge himself with this delightful meal. He looked up to take a breath of air and noticed that he was 100 yards from a waterfall and that the ice was moving rapidly toward the waterfall. But instead of flying away, he kept eating, though keeping his eye on the waterfall. At 25 yards he decided to take one last bite. Then at 10 yards he took one last mouthful. With only a few feet to go before the falls he tried to fly, but his feet were now frozen to the ice, and he tumbled to his death over the falls.

What important message does this story teach us about making decisions?

....

....

....

....

....

....

....

....

IN THE WORD

CHOOSING THE NARROW GATE

Read Matthew 7:13,14.

Choosing Which Way to Go

What choice does Jesus command before He even describes the options?

....

....

What makes the wide gate so popular?

....

....

What do you think the result of the wide gate, *destruction*, looks like?

....

....

Read John 10:9,10. In what position does Jesus place Himself?

....

....

What is the result of going through Jesus' gate?

....

....

Read Matthew 7:14 and John 10:10. What does Jesus mean by having life "to the full"?

....

....

The Road Less Traveled

Read John 14:1-6. "Where are we going? I don't know, do you? Who's going to lead the expedition?" You can hear the words of Thomas as he asks Jesus for directions (see v. 5).

Why do you think so few people choose the narrow gate?

....

....

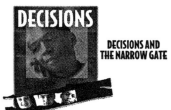

Read Deuteronomy 30:15-20. What options are listed for the Israelites?

....

....

What final command does Moses give in verse 19?

....

....

So What?
Decide to Live, Don't Live to Decide.

Many people are procrastinators when it comes to making decisions. Some people have allowed their procrastination to cause them to take the "wide road that leads to destruction." Remember, not deciding to live for Jesus is a decision!

Complete these sentences:

The biggest decisions weighing on my shoulders are...

....

....

I would make better decisions if I would...

....

....

I am glad to be alive because...

....

....

Read the following statement; then rate yourself from one to ten (ten being highest).

When it comes to discipline, saying no to second best for the sake of having the best, I rate myself as a ....

Circle three of your responses to the following question:

The areas of my life that are most difficult to discipline are...

eating habits	speech
sleep patterns	study habits
handling money	relationships
sexuality	church attendance
thoughts	anger/moods
humor	criticism of others
prayer life	exercise
sarcastic tongue	habit of backbiting
other:	

THINGS TO THINK ABOUT

1. What are roadblocks to making good decisions?

....
....
....

2. If you knew your life would be shortened, what would you do differently?

....
....
....

3. What is one decision you need to give to Christ?

....
....
....

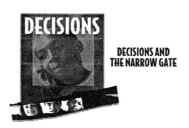

DECISIONS AND
THE NARROW GATE

 PARENT PAGE

LIFE'S TOO SHORT FOR BAD DECISIONS

One day when I was caught up in the tyranny of the urgent, a friend of mine sent me some thoughts entitled, "Things That Life Is Too Short For." Here are a few of those special thoughts:

- Life is too short to nurse grudges or hurt feelings.
- It's too short to worry about getting ready for Christmas. Just let Christmas come.
- It's too short to keep all your floors shiny.
- It's too short to let a day pass without hugging your loved ones.
- It's too short not to take a nap when you need one.
- It's too short to put off Bible study.
- It's too short to give importance to whether the towels match the bathroom.
- It's too short to miss the call to worship on a Sunday morning.
- It's too short to stay indoors on a crisp fall Saturday.
- It's too short to read all the junk mail.
- It's too short not to call or write your parents (or children) regularly.
- It's too short to work at a job you hate.
- It's too short not to stop and talk to children.
- It's too short to forget to pray.
- It's too short to put off improving your relationships with people you love.
- Life is just too short. Way too short to settle for mediocrity!

Now take a moment to list five personal "life-is-too-short-fors."

Life is too short for..

Life is too short for..

Life is too short for..

Life is too short for..

Life is too short for..

Now take time to share three more "life-is-too-short-for" phrases and this time have them geared to your family.

Life is too short for..

Life is too short for..

Life is too short for..

Session 10: "Decisions and the Narrow Gate"
Date...

GOOD FRUIT/BAD FRUIT;
GOOD PROPHET/BAD PROPHET

KEY VERSES

"'Watch out for false prophets. They come to you in sheep's clothing, but inwardly they are ferocious wolves. By their fruit you will recognize them. Do people pick grapes from thornbushes, or figs from thistles? Likewise every good tree bears good fruit, but a bad tree bears bad fruit. A good tree cannot bear bad fruit, and a bad tree cannot bear good fruit. Every tree that does not bear good fruit is cut down and thrown into the fire. Thus, by their fruit you will recognize them.'"
Matthew 7:15-20

BIBLICAL BASIS

Jeremiah 23:16;
Matthew 7:1,15-20; 24:24-28;
Galatians 5:22,23;
1 Timothy 6:3-5;
James 1:23-25;
2 Peter 2:1-3;
1 John 4:1-3

THE BIG IDEA

Beware of negative influences on your life. Look for the evidence of ungodliness in other people with whom you associate.

AIMS OF THIS SESSION

During this session you will guide students to:
• Examine the biblical concept of good and bad fruit and the difference between good and bad prophets;
• Discover the people and things that are both positive and negative influences in their own lives;
• Implement a plan to develop good spiritual fruit in their lives and to distinguish the positive and negative influences in their lives.

WARM UP

TASTE TEST—
Students fill in blanks with the names of foods.

TEAM EFFORT— JUNIOR HIGH/ MIDDLE SCHOOL

TRUE OR FALSE PROPHETS?—
Students decide whether or not some modern "prophets" are true or false.

TEAM EFFORT— HIGH SCHOOL

WHAT'S GOING ON?—
Students consider good and bad influences on their lives.

IN THE WORD

A TREE AND ITS FRUIT—
A Bible study on how to discern the good fruit from the bad and the true prophets from the false ones.

THINGS TO THINK ABOUT (OPTIONAL)

Questions to get students thinking and talking about positive and negative influences.

PARENT PAGE

A tool to get the session into the home and allow parents and young people to discuss how to bear good fruit.

DECISIONS

Leader's Devotional

"Anyone who listens to the word but does not do what it says is like a man who looks at his face in a mirror and, after looking at himself, goes away and immediately forgets what he looks like. But the man who looks intently into the perfect law that gives freedom, and continues to do this, not forgetting what he has heard, but doing it—he will be blessed in what he does" (James 1:23-25).

Flip on the television and you're up against MTV, Madonna, Pearl Jam, HBO, *NYPD*, and a legion of other violent, promiscuous messages. It doesn't matter what the medium is—TV, magazine, radio, film or even now the Internet—young people are surrounded by a seductive stream of false prophets. Teenagers are bombarded each day with message after message to do whatever feels right to them.

What makes youth ministry even more difficult is the question, "How can a youth worker stay pure in the midst of receiving the same messages?" Whether paid or volunteer, even as youth workers we are also subject to temptation by what we hear and see. Society influences us just as much as it does young people. That's why this lesson on discerning good fruit from bad fruit and good prophets from bad prophets is critical to our relationships with God—for teenager and youth worker alike.

Just as a small, young David took on a huge, ugly, God-profaning Goliath, as Christians we have the Lord who goes before us in battle. God is on our side. Our enemy is not Hollywood, television or the producers of the sick and twisted messages we hear and see everyday. Our enemy is Satan and our mission is to pray for the Holy Spirit to transform hearts.

This lesson will provide a fantastic launch pad to discuss all the hot issues and topics young people are confronted with every day. You can be sure that the wisdom in God's word will provide you just what you need to walk in a way that honors Him. God's word will supply you with the wisdom, discernment, protection, knowledge, understanding—everything the Holy Spirit uses—to produce good and lasting fruit in your life. (Written by Joey O'Connor.)

"Of two evils, choose neither."
—Charles Spurgeon

GOOD FRUIT/BAD FRUIT; GOOD PROPHET/BAD PROPHET

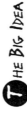

KEY VERSES

"Watch out for false prophets. They come to you in sheep's clothing, but inwardly they are ferocious wolves. By their fruit you will recognize them. Do people pick grapes from thorn-bushes, or figs from thistles? Likewise every good tree bears good fruit, but a bad tree bears bad fruit. A good tree cannot bear bad fruit, and a bad tree cannot bear good fruit. Every tree that does not bear good fruit is cut down and thrown into the fire. Thus, by their fruit you will recognize them.'" Matthew 7:15-20

BIBLICAL BASIS

Jeremiah 23:16; Matthew 7:1,15-20; 24:24-28; John 15:5; Galatians 5:22,23; 1 Timothy 6:3-5; James 1:23-25; 2 Peter 2:1-3

THE BIG IDEA

Beware of negative influences on your life. Look for the evidence of ungodliness in other people with whom you associate.

WARM UP (5-10 MINUTES)

TASTE TEST

• Divide students into pairs.
• Give each pair a copy of "Taste Test" on page 131 and a pen or pencil.
• Have students complete the page with their partners.
• Answers: 1. Lettuce, 2. Turkey, 3. Bread, 4. Apple, 5. Grease, 6. Corn, 7. Cauliflower, 8. Tea, 9. Carrot, 10. Pie (r-squared) 11. Salt, 12. Pear, 13. Butter, 14. Squash, 15. Meat, 16. Pepper, 17. Peas, 18. Beef, 19. Turnip, 20. Bacon, 21. Raisin, 22. Prune

Fold

		Positive
Susie Smith	Strong Christian influence	Negative
Sam Jones	Partying/peer pressure	

Circle two of the following sentence completions which apply to you:
For me to be better prepared to react properly to the false prophets, I need to...
a. pray for God's discernment.
b. ask for advice from a godly person.
c. choose my friends more carefully.
d. learn more about the truth in God's word so I can recognize what is false.
e. give up some of the "false prophets" in my life.
f. speak up for God's truth more often.
g. take the idea of evil and false prophets more seriously.

So WHAT?

Complete the following sentences:
The most negative influence in my life right now is...
....

The most positive influence in my life right now is...
....

THINGS TO THINK ABOUT (OPTIONAL)

• Use the questions on page 135 after, or as a part of "In the Word."
1. Why do you think Jesus included a warning about false prophets in the *Sermon on the Mount*?
....

2. Why is it often difficult to distinguish between good fruit and bad fruit or true prophets and false prophets?
....

3. What elements make good fruit go bad?
....

PARENT PAGE

• Distribute page to parents.

TEAM EFFORT—JUNIOR HIGH/MIDDLE SCHOOL (15-20 MINUTES)

TRUE OR FALSE PROPHETS?

- Bring in several magazines and newspapers, tape and scissors.
- Take two sheets of paper and on one print the word "True," on the other one print the word "False." Tape the two signs to a wall or board.
- Hand out the magazines and newspapers and ask the group to find and identify modern prophets for each category. Cut (or tear) out the pictures and tape them to the wall or board under the correct sign.
- Have the students discuss their findings.

TEAM EFFORT—HIGH SCHOOL (15-20 MINUTES)

WHAT'S GOIN' ON?

- Provide a bowl with a variety of fruit for observation by your group. Have each person select a fruit that best describes his or her relationship with Jesus at the present time.
- Give each student a copy of "What's Goin' On?" on page 132 and a pen or pencil.
- Divide students into pairs. Have the students complete the sheet below and discuss with their partner what's going on in their lives.

Read Matthew 7:15-20.

List the fruit (characteristics) you are bearing in your own life. Discuss your lists with your partner.

Good things goin' on in my relationship with Jesus	Not-so-good things goin' on in my relationship with Jesus

Conclude this time by praying for one another.

IN THE WORD (25-30 MINUTES)

A TREE AND ITS FRUIT

- Divide students into groups of three or four.
- Give each student a copy of "A Tree and Its Fruit" on pages 133, 134 and 135 and a pen or pencil, or display the page using an overhead projector.
- Have students complete the Bible study.

Read Matthew 7:15-20.

THE SPIRITUAL MASQUERADE PARTY

What do you think Jesus means by wolves in sheep's clothing?

--- Fold ---

According to Jesus, knowing the difference between good and bad fruit is vital for every believer. What other insights about true and false prophets can you gather from the following verses?

Jeremiah 23:16 ....

Matthew 24:24-28 ....

1 Timothy 6:3-5 ....

2 Peter 2:1-3 ....

1 John 4:1-3 ....

Why do you think Jesus included a warning on false prophets in the Sermon on the Mount?

What are some of the reasons people follow popular leaders and celebrities?

Jesus said that false prophets "come to you in sheep's clothing" (Matthew 7:15). His word picture was understood very well by the people of His day who were very familiar with sheep and shepherds. The picture He created was that of a very wily, dangerous animal disguised as a sweet, non-threatening animal. What disguise might false prophets wear today?

THE TRUE OR FALSE PROPHETS TEST

How can Galatians 5:22,23 help you determine the quality of a person's fruit (characteristics)?

How can you evaluate a person's fruit and still remain consistent with Jesus' words in Matthew 7:1?

In John 15:5 Jesus gave His followers an instruction. How will following this command help you to bear fruit?

FINDING THE TRUE AND FALSE PROPHETS IN MY WORLD

We all have people in our lives who are good influences and some who are bad influences. Who are the people who influence you?

Take a moment to think about who is influencing you and in what ways they are influencing. Then fill in the following chart. (You may list friends, family members, pastors, celebrities, teachers, etc.)

Name	How He or She Influences Me	Positive/Negative/So-So
Examples:		

GOOD FRUIT/BAD
FRUIT; GOOD
PROPHET/BAD
PROPHET

WARM UP

TASTE TEST[1]

1. "Hurry, dear. .... be going."

2. Istanbul is in ....

3. "Say, I'm broke, man. Can you loan me a little .... ?"

4. The .... achian mountains are beautiful in the Fall.

5. The Parthenon is in ....

6. I have a .... on my big toe.

7. Some prizefighters have .... ears.

8. The 20th letter of the alphabet is ....

9. Some people just don't .... all about the environment.

10. .... is found in the area of a circle.

11. "You are the .... of the earth."

12. Two of a kind is a ....

13. She wanted to buy it, ... husband said, "No."

14. If you step on a tomato, you might .... it.

15. "I'll .... you on the corner at 6:30 sharp."

16. "She's been a little sluggish, so I tried to .... up."

17. " .... on earth, goodwill toward men."

18. "Okay, just what is your .... ?"

19. Kids always .... their noses at foods that they don't like.

20. At Waikiki, you'll find many people .... in the sun.

21. Adam and Eve were busy .... Cain.

22. Every year, good gardeners will .... their trees.

Note:

1. Adapted from *Ideas Number 13-16* (El Cajon, Calif.: Youth Specialties, 1981), pp. 56-57.

TEAM EFFORT

WHAT'S GOIN' ON

Read Matthew 7:15-20.

List the fruit (characteristics) you are bearing in your own life. Discuss your lists with your partner.

Good things goin' on in my relationship with Jesus	Not-so-good things goin' on in my relationship with Jesus
....	....
....	....
....	....
....	....

Conclude this time by praying for one another.

GOOD FRUIT/BAD
FRUIT; GOOD
PROPHET/BAD
PROPHET

A TREE AND ITS FRUIT
Read Matthew 7:15-20.

The Spiritual Masquerade Party

What do you think Jesus means by wolves in sheep's clothing?

....

....

According to Jesus, knowing the difference between good and bad fruit is vital for every believer. What other insights about true and false prophets can you gather from the following verses?

Jeremiah 23:16 ....

....

Matthew 24:24-28 ....

....

1 Timothy 6:3-5 ....

....

2 Peter 2:1-3 ....

....

1 John 4:1-3 ....

....

Why do you think Jesus included a warning on false prophets in the Sermon on the Mount?

....

....

What are some of the reasons people follow popular leaders and celebrities?

....

....

IN THE WORD

Jesus said that false prophets "come to you in sheep's clothing" (Matthew 7:15). His word picture was understood very well by the people of His day who were very familiar with sheep and shepherds. The picture He created was that of a very wily, dangerous animal disguised as a sweet, non-threatening animal.

What disguises might false prophets wear today?

....

....

The True or False Prophets Test

How can Galatians 5:22,23 help you determine the quality of a person's fruit (characteristics)?

....

....

....

How can you evaluate a person's fruit and still remain consistent with Jesus' words in Matthew 7:1?

....

....

....

In John 15:5 Jesus gave His followers an instruction. How will following this command help you to bear fruit?

....

....

Finding the True and False Prophets in My World

We all have people in our lives who are good influences and some who are bad influences. Who are the people who influence you?

Take a moment to think about who is influencing you and in what ways they are influencing you. Then fill in the following chart. (You may list friends, family members, pastors, celebrities, teachers, etc.)

Name	How He or She Influences Me	Positive/Negative/So-So
Examples:		
Susie Smith	Strong Christian influence	Positive
Sam Jones	Partying/peer pressure	Negative

....

....

....

....

....

IN THE WORD

Circle two of the following sentence completions which apply to you:

For me to be better prepared to react properly to the false prophets, I need to...

a. pray for God's discernment.

b. ask for advice from a godly person.

c. choose my friends more carefully.

d. learn more about the truth in God's word so I can recognize what is false.

e. give up some of the "false prophets" in my life.

f. speak up for God's truth more often.

g. take the idea of evil and false prophets more seriously.

So What?

Complete the following sentences:

The most negative influence in my life right now is...

....

....

The most positive influence in my life right now is...

....

....

THINGS TO THINK ABOUT

1. Why do you think Jesus included a warning about false prophets in the Sermon on the Mount?

....

....

2. Why is it often difficult to distinguish between good fruit and bad fruit or true prophets and false prophets?

....

....

3. What elements make good fruit go bad?

....

....

DECISIONS

GOOD FRUIT/BAD
FRUIT; GOOD
PROPHET/BAD
PROPHET

PARENT PAGE

BEARING GOOD FRUIT

"Every tree that does not bear good fruit is cut down and thrown into the fire" (Matthew 7:19).

How can this warning to false prophets also keep us from becoming complacent as Christians?

....

....

What action steps can you take to insure that you will bear good fruit?

....

....

In case you ever get discouraged in the "bearing fruit" department of your life, here is a great story to give you reassurance that God will help you with your spiritual growth. Don't give up!

Ignace Jan Paderewski, the famous composer-pianist, was scheduled to perform at a great concert hall in America. It was an evening to remember—black tuxedos and long evening dresses, a high society extravaganza. Present in the audience that evening was a mother with her fidgety nine-year-old son. Weary of waiting, he squirmed constantly in his seat. His mother was in hopes that her boy would be encouraged to practice the piano if he could just hear the immortal Paderewski at the keyboard. So—against his wishes—he had come.

As she turned to talk with friends, her son could stay seated no longer. He slipped away from her side, strangely drawn to the ebony concert Steinway and its leather tufted stool on the huge stage flooded with blinding lights. Without much notice from the sophisticated audience, the boy sat down at the stool, staring wide-eyed at the black and white keys. He placed his small, trembling fingers in the right location and began to play "Chopsticks." The roar of the crowd was hushed as hundreds of frowning faces turned in his direction. Irritated and embarrassed, they began to shout:

Session 11: "Good Fruit/ Bad Fruit;
Good Prophet/ Bad Prophet"
Date...

PARENT PAGE

"Get that boy away from there!"

"Who'd bring a kid that young in here?"

"Where's his mother?"

"Somebody stop him!"

Backstage, the master overheard the sounds out front and quickly put together in his mind what was happening. Hurriedly, he grabbed his coat and rushed toward the stage. Without one word of announcement, he stooped over behind the boy, reached around both sides, and began to improvise a counter melody to harmonize with and enhance "Chopsticks." As the two of them played together, Paderewski kept whispering in the boy's ear:

"Keep going. Don't quit, son. Keep on playing...don't stop...don't quit."

And so it is with us. We continue to work on our spiritual lives and God improvises on our behalf. He provides just the right touch at just the right moment.[1]

How does this story relate to you?

....

....

....

Note:

1. Source unknown.

THE TRUE FOUNDATION

KEY VERSES

"'Therefore everyone who hears these words of mine and puts them into practice is like a wise man who built his house on the rock. The rain came down, the streams rose, and the winds blew and beat against that house; yet it did not fall, because it had its foundation on the rock. But everyone who hears these words of mine and does not put them into practice is like a foolish man who built his house on the sand. The rain came down, the streams rose, and the winds blew and beat against that house, and it fell with a great crash.'" Matthew 7:24-27

BIBLICAL BASIS

Deuteronomy 32:4;
Proverbs 12:15-20;
Matthew 7:21-29;
James 1:22;
Revelation 3:15,16

THE BIG IDEA

True Christianity is found in calling Jesus "Lord" and by hearing and obeying His words.

AIMS OF THIS SESSION

During this session you will guide students to:
- Examine how to make Christ the Lord of their life;
- Discover how to properly prepare for the storms of life that will come into their lives;
- Implement a commitment to build their faith on the rock, which is the Lordship of Jesus Christ.

WARM UP

BARNYARD—
A game to liven up the group.

TEAM EFFORT— JUNIOR HIGH/ MIDDLE SCHOOL

THE PRESSURE TEST—
Students discover how much pressure they can stand.

TEAM EFFORT— HIGH SCHOOL

FINISH THAT STORY—
Students give two different endings to stories.

IN THE WORD

THE WISE AND FOOLISH BUILDERS—
A Bible study on building lives with the right foundation—Jesus Christ.

THINGS TO THINK ABOUT (OPTIONAL)

Questions to get students thinking and talking about strengthening the foundations of their own lives.

PARENT PAGE

A tool to get the session into the home and allow parents and young people to discuss how to do God's will.

DECISIONS

LEADER'S DEVOTIONAL

"He is the Rock, his works are perfect, and all his ways are just. A faithful God who does no wrong, upright and just is he" (Deuteronomy 32:4).

Why does the Sermon on the Mount end with the crowds in amazement at the teachings of Jesus? The only clue we are given is that the final verse states Jesus "taught as one who had authority, and not as their teachers of the law" (Matthew 7:29). Isn't it interesting that the common people were not amazed or impressed with the current religious leaders and that the teachers of the law obviously did not have the respect of the people. Why? Because they didn't teach with authority, nor did they back up their teaching with their lives.

The people's acceptance of His authority shows there was a very close relationship between the actual words of Jesus and how He lived His life. The people were amazed with Jesus and His words because He lived with integrity. Not only was Jesus' message transforming, so was His life. I think there's a very clear message here for all of us who work with teenagers.

Young people today are searching, but they're also skeptical. Yes, many of them have problems with authority, primarily because the authorities in their lives haven't done much to gain their respect. Teenagers today also aren't very impressed with most religious leaders. They don't want to hear about developing a "true foundation" for their lives; they want to see a true foundation alive and working in *your* life.

Young people today desperately want to believe in something—someone greater than themselves—but they also don't want to be embarrassed or made fools of. They want to be amazed. They want to live for a higher purpose. And yes, they want and need someone with authority to help them navigate the difficult, stormy seas of adolescence.

You have the awesome privilege of communicating the amazing words of Jesus to teenagers. As an authority in their lives, you don't have to be perfect—just authentic and real. Young people are looking for a solid foundation for their lives. You are just the person to model for them the true foundation God has laid in your life.
(Written by Joey O'Connor.)

"Let us endeavor so to live that when we come to die even the undertaker will be sorry."—Anonymous

THE TRUE FOUNDATION

EY VERSES

K EY VERSES

"Therefore everyone who hears these words of mine and puts them into practice is like a wise man who built his house on the rock. The rain came down, the streams rose, and the winds blew and beat against that house; yet it did not fall, because it had its foundation on the rock. But everyone who hears these words of mine and does not put them into practice is like a foolish man who built his house on the sand. The rain came down, the streams rose, and the winds blew and beat against that house, and it fell with a great crash." Matthew 7:24-27

B IBLICAL BASIS

Deuteronomy 32:4; Proverbs 12:15-20; Matthew 7:21-29; James 1:22; Revelation 3:15,16

T HE BIG IDEA

True Christianity is found in calling Jesus "Lord" and by hearing and obeying His words.

W ARM UP (5-10 MINUTES)

BARNYARD

- Before the session prepare enough slips of paper for each student to have one of the following six animals written on his or her slip of paper: Pig, Horse, Cow, Chicken, Duck and Dog.
- Fold each slip of paper and, as you hand them out, instruct students not to look at his or her paper or to show it to anyone else in the room. Also, as you hand the papers out, make sure that you hand out each of the six animal names in equal portions to insure equal teams.
- Instruct students to look at their slips of paper without letting others see what is on them. Tell them that as soon as you have turned out the lights, they must each begin to make the sound of that animal and then try to find other members of the same animal team, lock arms with their team members and continue to find their other team members.
- After a few minutes, turn the lights back on and tell everyone to remain in their groups. The winning team is the one with the most complete team.
- Option: Give one person in the group a slip of paper with "donkey" written on it. He or she will wander around looking for more donkeys without any luck at all. As compensation for being the only "donkey," you might want to give that person a prize for being (hopefully) a good sport.

Fold

In what areas of your life do you still need to allow Him lordship?

PREPARE FOR THE STORM OF LIFE

We need to get this straight: Rain, wind and storms come to everyone's lives. Christians are not exempt from pain and trouble. The question is, "How will you handle the pressures that come your way?"

What happens to you when the pressures of life come? To examine this question better, first think about what has caused worry, trouble or strain in your life. Circle five things on the following list that you see as pressures in your life:

Death of someone close to you	Injury	Job
Grades	Money	College applications
Teachers	Moving	Responsibilities
Friends	Dating	Drugs and/or alcohol
Lack of dates	School tasks	Future
Holiday season	Nuclear war	Illness
Family	Debts	Other:

Where do you turn and what do you do when the storm hits?

Where?

What?

Remember this thought: Pressure reveals the person.

How much do you let the Lord be the foundation in your life during the storm? Mark the most appropriate answer on the following continuum and then give the reason for your answer in the space provided.

Always	Most Often	Sometimes	Seldom	Never

So WHAT?

In what area of your life do you need to let Jesus be Lord?

How will you obey Jesus in this area?

T HINGS TO THINK ABOUT (OPTIONAL)

- Use the questions on page 146 after or as a part of "In the Word."
1. Who in your life is an example of Christlike obedience?

2. Why do some people crumble during times of pressure?

3. What steps can you personally take to strengthen your foundation in Christ?

P ARENT PAGE

- Distribute page to parents.

TEAM EFFORT—JUNIOR HIGH/ MIDDLE SCHOOL (15-20 MINUTES)

THE PRESSURE TEST

- Ask for volunteers from the group.
- Create a "pressure test" by timing how long each person can withstand a certain activity. A few examples might be (you can definitely make up others):

  Ice cubes on the forehead

  Standing on his or her head

  Squatting with back against the wall without leg support

- Then discuss the pressures of life and how we all experience our breaking points.
- Ask "What are some of the biggest pressures you face in your life?"

TEAM EFFORT—HIGH SCHOOL (15-20 MINUTES)

FINISH THAT STORY

- Give each student a copy of "Finish That Story" on page 143 and a pen or pencil.
- Divide students into groups of three or four. Assign Bill's story to half of the groups, and Carrie's story to the other half of the groups.
- Have the groups complete their assigned stories and then share their endings with the whole group.

Read Matthew 7:21-29. Then read the story assigned to your group and complete the story with two different endings.

Ending one: The story of building his or her foundation on the sand.

Ending two: The story of building his or her foundation on the rock.

BILL'S STORY

Ending One: Building his life upon sand

Ending Two: Building his life on the rock

CARRIE'S STORY

Ending One: Building her life upon sand

Ending Two: Building her life on the rock

IN THE WORD (25-30 MINUTES)

THE WISE AND FOOLISH BUILDERS

- Divide students into groups of three or four.
- Give each student a copy of "The Wise and Foolish Builders" on pages 144, 145 and 146

---- Fold ----

and a pen or pencil, or display the page using an overhead projector.

- Have students complete the Bible study.

BUT LORD, LORD—MATTHEW 7:21-23

Read Matthew 7:21-23.

Jesus mentioned someone who cried, "Lord, Lord," but who lacked commitment to Him. What point is Jesus making in this passage?

Why does Jesus place so much importance on obedience?

What does it mean "to do the will of my Father" (v. 21)?

Why do you think Jesus ends the Sermon on the Mount with an emphasis on hearing and doing?

How does James 1:22 reinforce these words of Jesus?

ACTIONS SPEAK LOUDER THAN WORDS—MATTHEW 7:24-29

Read Matthew 7:24-29.

How would you summarize the parable of the two houses?

Jesus compared wisdom and foolishness and so did many of the Old Testament writers. What characteristics of wisdom and foolishness are found in Proverbs 12:15-20?

Wisdom   Foolishness

How does Matthew 7:24-29 provide a fitting conclusion to the Sermon on the Mount?

MAKE CHRIST THE LORD OF YOUR LIFE

Jesus states that many call Him "Lord" but neglect to make Him Lord. When it comes to calling Jesus "Lord of your life," what are you really saying?

a. "My Lord and My God"

b. "My Rescuer in a time of trouble"

c. "My Good Buddy"

d. "The same thing everybody else is saying"

e. "My parents' Lord"

f. "The Cop in the sky"

g. "A Supreme Being"

h. "The Great Killjoy"

i. "_____"

The word "lord" means "master." Jesus wants to be the Master of our lives. In what ways have you given Him control of your life?

**THE TRUE
FOUNDATION**

FINISH THAT STORY

Read Matthew 7:21-29. Then read the story assigned to your group and complete the story with two different endings.

Ending one: The story of building his or her foundation on the sand.

Ending two: The story of building his or her foundation on the rock.

Bill's Story

Bill's father was an alcoholic and his mother was not a Christian. All the rest of Bill's brothers and sisters (five including Bill) had basically partied through high school, gotten jobs that were less than exciting and were on the road to destruction. Bill was the youngest. In actuality he didn't have a good role model in the entire family. Yet for some reason he seemed different. He wasn't the partyer the others were and he had so far done well in school.

Ending One: Building his life upon sand.

....

....

Ending Two: Building his life on the rock.

....

....

Carrie's Story

Carrie came from a Christian home. She had done all the "normal" teenage rebellious stuff. Carrie basically lived two separate lives: her life at church and her life at school. Sometimes she felt guilty and was convicted about her worldly lifestyle at school, but she didn't really feel compelled to change.

At a Christian camp the speaker read the Scripture: "'I know your deeds, that you are neither cold nor hot. I wish you were either one or the other! So, because you are lukewarm—neither hot nor cold—I am about to spit you out of my mouth'" (Revelation 3:15,16).

Carrie knew she was lukewarm.

Ending One: Building her life upon sand.

....

....

Ending Two: Building her life on the rock.

....

....

IN THE WORD

THE WISE AND FOOLISH BUILDERS

This ending to the Sermon on the Mount is a challenge to live out the message of this great exhortation. The words are simple, the message is clear, the truth is found in these powerful words.

But Lord, Lord—Matthew 7:21-23

Read Matthew 7:21-23.

Jesus mentioned someone who cried, "Lord, Lord," but who lacked commitment to Him. What point is Jesus making in this passage?

....

Why does Jesus place so much importance on obedience?

....

What does it mean "to do the will of my Father" (v. 21)?

....

Why do you think Jesus ends the Sermon on the Mount with an emphasis on hearing and doing?

....

How does James 1:22 reinforce these words of Jesus?

....

Actions Speak Louder than Words—Matthew 7:24-29

Read Matthew 7:24-29.

How would you summarize the parable of the two houses?

....

Jesus compared wisdom and foolishness and so did many of the Old Testament writers. What characteristics of wisdom and foolishness are found in Proverbs 12:15-20?

Wisdom

....

Foolishness

....

....

How does Matthew 7:24-29 provide a fitting conclusion to the Sermon on the Mount?

....

THE TRUE
FOUNDATION

 N THE WORD

Make Christ the Lord of Your Life

Jesus states that many call Him Lord but neglect to make Him Lord. When it comes to calling Jesus Lord of your life, what are you really saying?

a. "My Lord and My God"
b. "My Rescuer in a time of trouble"
c. "My Good Buddy"
d. "The same thing everybody else is saying"
e. "My parents' Lord"
f. "The Cop in the sky"
g. "A Supreme Being"
h. "The Great Killjoy"
i. "..."

The word "lord" means "master." Jesus wants to be the Master of our lives. In what ways have you given Him control of your life?

....

....

In what areas of your life do you still need to allow Him lordship?

....

....

Prepare for the Storm of Life

We need to get this straight: Rain, wind and storms come to everyone's lives. Christians are not exempt from pain and trouble. The question is, "How will you handle the pressures that come your way?"

What happens to you when the pressures of life come? To examine this question better, first think about what has caused worry, trouble or strain in your life. Circle five things on the following list that you see as pressures in your life:

Death of someone close to you	Injury	Job
Grades	Money	College applications
Teachers	Moving	Responsibilities
Friends	Dating	Drugs and/or alcohol
Lack of dates	School tasks	Future
Holiday season	Nuclear war	Illness
Family	Debts	Other:

Where do you turn and what do you do when the storm hits?

Where? ....

What? ....

IN THE WORD

Remember this thought: Pressure reveals the person.

How much do you let the Lord be the foundation in your life during the storm? Circle the most appropriate answer on the following continuum and then give the reason for your answer in the space provided.

Always	Most Often	Sometimes	Seldom	Never

....

....

So What?
In what area of your life do you need to let Jesus be Lord?

....

....

How will you obey Jesus in this area?

....

....

THINGS TO THINK ABOUT

1. Who in your life is an example of Christlike obedience?

....

....

2. Why do some people crumble during times of pressure?

....

....

3. What steps can you personally take to strengthen your foundation in Christ?

....

....

PARENT **P**AGE

DECISIONS

THE TRUE FOUNDATION

LET CHRIST HAVE AUTHORITY IN YOUR LIFE

"When Jesus had finished saying these things, the crowds were amazed at his teaching, because he taught as one who had authority, and not as their teachers of the law" (Matthew 7:28,29).

The people were amazed that Jesus taught with such authority. How do you react to the authority of Jesus in your life? Circle one of the following phrases that best describes you:

1. I, too, am amazed.
2. He's the boss.
3. I think He has to compete with me.
4. My submission to His rule comes and goes.
5. To be honest, He loses out to my will.
6. He seems to play second string on my team.

Dr. James Dobson tells a great story about a little obnoxious boy who was very disobedient.

Robert arrived in the dental office, prepared for battle.

"Get in the chair, young man," said the doctor.

"No chance!" replied the boy.

"Son, I told you to climb onto the chair and that's what I intend for you to do," said the dentist.

Robert stared at his opponent for a moment and then replied, "If you make me get in that chair, I will take off all my clothes."

The dentist calmly said, "Son, take 'em off."

The boy forthwith removed his shirt, undershirt, shoes and socks, and then looked up in defiance.

"All right son," said the dentist. "Now get in the chair."

"You didn't hear me," sputtered Robert. "I said if you make me get in that chair, I will take off all my clothes."

"Son, take 'em off," replied the man.

Robert proceeded to remove his pants and shorts, finally standing totally naked before the dentist and his assistant.

"Now son, get in the chair," said the doctor.

Robert did as he was told, and sat cooperatively through the entire procedure. When the cavities were drilled and filled, he was instructed to step down from the chair.

"Give me my clothes now," said the boy.

"I'm sorry," replied the dentist. "Tell your mother that we're

Session 12: "The True Foundation"
Date.................................

going to keep your clothes tonight. She can pick them up tomorrow."

Can you comprehend the shock Robert's mother received when the door to the waiting room opened, and there stood her pink son, as naked as the day he was born? The room was filled with patients, but Robert and his mom walked past them and into the hall. They went down a public elevator and into the parking lot, ignoring the snickers of onlookers.

The next day, Robert's mother returned to retrieve his clothes, and asked to have a word with the dentist. However, she did not come to protest. These were her sentiments: "You don't know how much I appreciate what happened here yesterday. You see, Robert has been blackmailing me about his clothes for years...If I don't immediately buy him what he wants, he threatens to take off all his clothes. You are the first person who has called his bluff, doctor, and the impact on Robert has been incredible."[1]

The dentist called the boy's bluff and the result was interesting, to say the least. What would happen if Jesus called your bluff if you were calling out, "Lord, Lord"? Circle the most appropriate answer.

1. I'd be caught living a lie.
2. He'd see me giving it my best.
3. It depends on the time and the place.
4. I would be happy to receive His insight.
5. It would really scare me.
6. Other:

Complete this sentence:

The way for me to not only say "Lord, Lord," but to also do His will is...

....

....

Note:

1. Dr. James Dobson, *Straight Talk to Men and Their Wives* (Waco: Word Books, 1980), pp. 58-60.

Add a New Member to Your Youth Staff.

Jim Burns is President of the National Institute of Youth Ministry.

Meet Jim Burns. He won't play guitar and he doesn't do windows, but he will take care of your programming needs. That's because his new curriculum, **YouthBuilders Group Bible Studies,** is a comprehensive program designed to take your group through their high school years. (If you have junior high kids in your group, **YouthBuilders** works for them too.)

For less than $6 a month you'll get Jim Burns's special recipe of high-involvement, discussion-oriented, Bible-centered studies. It's the next generation of Bible curriculum for youth—and with Jim on your staff, you'll be free to spend more time one-on-one with the kids in your group.

Here are some of YouthBuilders' hottest features:

- Reproducible pages—one book fits your whole group
- Wide appeal—big groups, small groups—even adjusts to combine junior high/high school groups
- Hits home—special section to involve parents with every session of the study
- Interactive Bible discovery—geared to help young people find answers themselves
- Cheat sheets—a Bible *Tuck-In*™ with all the session information on a single page
- Flexible format—perfect for Sunday mornings, midweek youth meetings, or camps and retreats
- Three studies in one—each study has three four-session modules that examine critical life choices.

   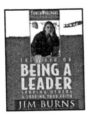   

The Word on Sex, Drugs & Rock 'N' Roll
Gives youth a biblical framework for making good choices in life.
ISBN 08307.16424
$16.99

The Word on Prayer and the Devotional Life
Help youth get closer to God by getting a grip on prayer.
ISBN 08307.16432
$16.99

The Word on the Basics of Christianity
Here are the foundational truths of Christianity, presented in an active format.
ISBN 08307.16440
$16.99

The Word on Being a Leader, Serving Others & Sharing Your Faith
Students can serve God and each other by taking an active role in leadership.
ISBN 08307.16459
$16.99

The Word on Helping Friends in Crisis
Young people can discover what God's Word says about crisis issues and how to help others.
ISBN 08307.16467
$16.99

The Word on the Life of Jesus
Students examine Christ's life–from birth, the gathering of the disciples, death and resurrection to His second coming.
Manual
ISBN08307.16475
$16.99

The Word on Finding and Using Your Spiritual Gifts
Show teens what spiritual gifts are and how they can discover and use their own spiritual gifts.
Manual
ISBN 08307.17897
$16.99

More Great Resources from Jim Burns

Drugproof Your Kids
Stephen Arterburn and Jim Burns
Solid biblical principles are combined with the most effective prevention and intervention techniques to give parents a guide they can trust.
ISBN 08307.17714 • $10.99

90 Days Through the New Testament
Jim Burns
A 90-day growth experience through the New Testament that lays the foundation for developing a daily time with God.
ISBN 08307.14561 • $9.99

The Youth Worker's Book of Case Studies
Jim Burns
Fifty-two true stories with discussion questions to add interest to Bible studies.
ISBN 08307.15827
$12.99

Drugproof Your Kids Video A 90-minute seminar featuring Stephen Arterburn and Jim Burns. Includes a reproducible syllabus.
SPCN 85116.00876 • $19.99

For more great resources and to learn about leadership training, please see other side.

Gospel Light

Youth Ministry Resources from Gospel Light.

Give Your Young People the Victory.

Here is the powerful message of Neil Anderson's best-selling book, *Victory over the Darkness,* written especially for young people. *Stomping Out the Darkness* provides junior high through high school youth with the keys they are desperately searching for—keys to their identities, worth, significance, security and acceptance as children of God.

Stomping Out the Darkness
Neil T. Anderson and Dave Park
Trade • ISBN 08307.16408

Jim Burns Shows Youth Radical Alternatives to the World.

Radical Love
Help teens make godly choices with the Christian approach to love, sex and dating.
Trade • ISBN 08307.17935
Video • SPCN 85116.00922

Radical Christianity
How to make your life count for the ultimate cause—Jesus Christ!
Trade • ISBN 08307.17927

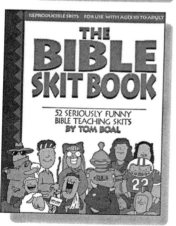

Bible Skits for All Occasions.

Here's a great way to get your kids out of their seats and into the Word. *The Bible Skit Book* gives you 52 lively, reproducible Bible-theme skits. Each skit includes director's tips, accurate Bible background information and group discussion questions. Great for camps, clubs and sermon illustrations, too. Less than 33¢ per skit!

The Bible Skit Book
Tom Boal
Manual • ISBN 08307.16238

A Support Group for Parents of Teens.

This seven-session course focuses on biblical principles of parenting, and explains seven building blocks to becoming an effective parent.

"Hi, I'm Bob and I'm the Parent of a Teenager."
Tim Smith
Manual • ISBN 08307.14650

Faster than a Speeding Bulletin.

Break through solid walls of boredom to reach youth with this fun, new, high-quality clip art that will supercharge flyers and newsletters. Here are borders, mastheads and illustrations for everything from camping, games and summer events to worship and missions activities.

Super Clip Art for Youth Workers
Tom Finley
Manual • ISBN 08307.15177

Now available for your computer!
For IBM or Mac

Ask Your Students the Questions that "Hit Home."

Fifty true case studies, compiled by Jim Burns, pose real-life moral questions to teenagers for group discussion and learning. Scripture references and discussion questions included.

The Youth Worker's Book of Case Studies
Jim Burns
Manual • ISBN 08307.15827

To order these and other Gospel Light youth resources contact your Gospel Light supplier, or call 1-800-4-GOSPEL. **Gospel Light**

What in the world is *NIYM*?

- A.) The Neurotically Inclined Yo-Yo Masters
- B.) The Neatest Incidental Yearbook Mystery
- C.) The Natural Ignition Yields of Marshmallows
- D.) The National Institute of Youth Ministry

If you deliberately picked *A*, *B*, or *C* you're the reason Jim Burns started NIYM! If you picked *D*, you can go to the next page. In any case, you could learn more about NIYM. Here are some IQ score-raisers:

Jim Burns started NIYM to:
- Meet the growing needs of training and equipping youth workers and parents
- Develop excellent resources and events for young people—in the U.S. and internationally
- Empower young people and their families to make wise decisions and experience a vital Christian lifestyle.

NIYM can make a difference in your life and enhance your youth work skills through these special events:

Institutes—These consist of week-long, in-depth small-group training sessions for youth workers.

Trainer of Trainees—NIYM will train you to train others. You can use this training with your volunteers, parents and denominational events. You can go through the certification process and become an official NIYM associate. (No, you don't get a badge or decoder ring).

International Training—Join NIYM associates to bring youth ministry to kids and adults around the world. (You'll learn meanings to universal words like "yo!" and "hey!")

Custom Training—These are special training events for denominational groups, churches, networks, colleges and seminaries.

Parent Forums—We'll come to your church or community with two incredible hours of learning, interaction and fellowship. It'll be fun finding out who makes your kids tick!

Youth Events—Dynamic speakers, interaction and drama bring a powerful message to kids through a fun and fast-paced day. Our youth events include: This Side Up, Radical Respect, Surviving Adolescence and Peer Leadership.

For brain food or a free information packet about the National Institute of Youth Ministry, write to:

NIYM

P.O. Box 4374 • San Clemente, CA 92674

Tel: (714) 498-4418 • Fax: (714) 498-0037 • NIYMin@aol.com